What It
Means to Be
Born
Again

Rev. Bruce Coats
November, 1994

What It Means to Be
Born Again

Johnnie C. Godwin

A BARBOUR BOOK

© Copyright MCMLXXVII by Broadman Press

ISBN 1-55748-542-9

Published by **BARBOUR AND COMPANY, INC.**
              P.O. BOX 719
              UHRICHSVILLE, OH 44683

Printed in the United States of America.

To

Phyllis

who for over twenty years

has helped me share with others

what it means to be born again

Foreword

It is important that some Christian intellectual should attempt to clarify the conception of rebirth. Since, from the time of Nicodemus, this experience has been puzzling to those who have not shared in it, we are not surprised that many are puzzled today. I am glad that there is appearing a book that is marked by clarity of thought, firmness of conviction, and simplicity of style. The style of the present work is admirably suited to its purpose because those who most need clarification appreciate a straightforward and uncomplicated approach. Very early in my career as an author, I realized that it is genuinely possible to express the most profound truths in fundamentally simple language. I saw that obscurity is not ordinarily a mark of profundity. The author of this book, I am glad to say, has not been afraid to be clear and concrete.

In a deep sense, the present volume is really devoted to commitment. This is necessary because a Christian is one who is committed to Jesus Christ! He is not one who claims to be righteous, but one who claims to be committed. It is this experience of commitment which brings a new center to a person's confused efforts and, in an astonishing number of instances, produces a really new character. The new character, being finite, can still make mistakes and actually does so; but that is not the primary fact. The primary fact is that all of the person's powers are employed in a new way and that his movements are dignified by a new direction. He is a wandering planet which becomes stable in its movements by entering a new orbit.

There is a greater difference between nominal Christianity and a fully committed Christianity than there is between paganism and a nominal attachment to Christian culture. Johnnie Godwin is writing about the second step, and this is the one of genuine magnitude.

D. Elton Trueblood

Preface

I wrote this book to help explain what it means to be born again. In recent days preachers have preached enough sermons on what it means to be born again to fill several books. The subject has been a part of religious and secular magazines and of television interviews. People are obviously intensely interested in knowing what it means to be born again. Along with the interest people have, there is a lot of misunderstanding and inaccurate information. The popular interest, the need for right answers, and my commitment to lead people to experience the new birth have led me to write this book. Of course, I am aware that no one book can tell everything the new birth means and all it implies. And I know that I have written out of my experience and perspective and that others would have taken a different approach. Still, I am trusting God to use the words in this book so that others will be able to answer the ultimate question with: "Yes, I have been born again; God has forgiven me of my sins; and I'm happier than I've ever been in my life."

In the first chapter I have focused on who is asking the question about being born again and why. From there I went on to trace the biblical source of the term, show some of the understandings through Christian history, and then explain changes that take place in the new birth experience.

I tried to stick with people talk—language that we use in everyday life—except for key terms that I tried to define as simply as I could. I have a firm conviction that no one need apologize for trying to state profound messages in simple language. Yet, language has its limitations. You will read about a man named Charles as you come to the last of the book. And as I came to the end of the book I felt as inadequate as I did when I left that friend born once but not twice. But it is encouraging to know that God can and does work through our limitations. And I hope that will be your experience as you read what I've written.

I'm grateful to all of the people who have helped in the writing of this book. I'm especially grateful to Dr. Grady C. Cothen for suggesting the book, to Dick Waters for designing the cover, and to Melody Gill for doing special research.

And thanks to you for wanting to know more about what it means to be born again.

—Genuinely,
Johnnie Godwin

Contents

1. Born Again?

DEAR ABBY: Please explain in easy pool-hall language just what people mean when they say they are "born again"—or "twice-born." Thank you.
                        B. H. : CLAY CITY, ILL.

More people than ever before seem to be asking what it means to be *born again*. And many people who aren't asking the question have a variety of thoughts about what the term means. Mixed in with accurate answers are a lot of wrong answers and wrong implications about what being born again means in the twentieth century.

Since the question is popular and since being born twice is the greatest thing that can happen to those who have been born once, this book seems to be needed. And we will see that even more clearly as we examine who is asking what it means to be born again.

13

Who's Asking?

From the one who wrote to "Dear Abby" in her
newspaper column, we can assume that people in the
pool hall want to know what it means to be born again.
Or, from the wording of the question, we at least know
that the writer wanted an answer in everyday people
talk that he could understand. He didn't care about
an answer in stained-glass language.

Abby's answer was fine. She said, "They mean
that they have accepted Jesus Christ as their personal
Savior, and have put their faith and trust in him." Although the answer was right, people in the pool hall
might like to have the details spelled out; and they
might like to know more about the experience of being
born again. This book will help them get a fuller
answer to their question—and in language they can understand.

People in other places want to know what it means
to be born again. A religion editor for a metropolitan
daily asked Dr. James L. Sullivan (1976 Southern
Baptist Convention President), "Who are these Baptists
and what does it mean to be 'born again'?" Later
Sullivan commented on his interviewer and the question: "He got it in nontheological terms, but he said,
'Well, thank you for helping me understand.' "

Politicians and people who are concerned about
politics want to know what it means to be born again.

People of various religions and different races want to know. And anyone who has a natural curiosity and hears of someone being born again wants to know the meaning of the term. But why all of the sudden interest in a term that is thousands of years old?

Why People Want to Know

Famous people are claiming that they have been born again. For example? Billy Graham, Charles Colson, and Jimmy Carter, to name just three who have caused others to want to know what it means to be born again. Along with these three, there are athletes, astronauts, scientists, entertainers, and people from almost every walk of life who claim to have been born again.

No one seemed to have minded hearing Billy Graham talk about being born again. And, in fact, multiplied thousands have joined Billy Graham in this experience by accepting his explanation and invitation to be born again. Billy Graham is an evangelist, so his religious talk is natural to his vocation. Although he is influential, he does not have personal authority over anyone; consequently, his beliefs are not a threat to people.

But what happens if a politician gets religion and claims to be born again? Charles Colson, who was a top presidential aide to Richard Nixon, was linked with the Watergate cover-up and served seven months

in prison. Before that he already wore the label of
being the hatchet man in the Nixon administration.
Yet, in the midst of scandal and trial, Charles Colson
had an experience that he described as being born
again.

Colson had begun to question the purpose of his
life and had come up with no real answers. Tom
Phillips, a friend and a new Christian himself, shared
the joy he had found in Christ and recommended that
Colson read C. S. Lewis' *Mere Christianity*. The influence of Phillips and of Colson's brother Harold,
combined with the powerful effect of Lewis' book,
led Charles Colson to become born again. Only in
the trying experiences of prison, however, did Colson
come to a deeper understanding of what it meant to
be born again.

Doubt and cynicism about Colson's experience
were natural responses to expect from multitudes of
people as they made judgments about his claim.
Under the circumstances, people doubted his motives
and his sincerity; and many simply misunderstood
what he claimed to have experienced. Through trial
and prison, though, Colson continued his claim. And
he wrote a book entitled *Born Again* (Old Tappan,
New Jersey: Chosen Books, 1976).

Charles Colson and his book focused on the term
born again. People began to read what Colson meant
by the term, and others heard him tell what he meant.

In preparation for this book, a researcher tried to get Colson's book at two metropolitan libraries, and at both the book was checked out. She went to a bookstore to get the book, and the book was sold out. Then she went to a branch library and found that neither of its copies of the book was available. When told she could get on the waiting list at the branch library, she asked how many people were ahead of her; and the librarian told her that twenty-one people were waiting to check out the book. The researcher finally found the book in another bookstore. Yes, people do want to know what it means to be born again; and they're especially interested when someone in politics has the experience.

An evangelist and a former political personality claim to be born again. But so what? They don't have any real power or authority over anyone's life. However, when a person of national prominence and potential power is involved, it is easy to understand why people would have an intense desire to know what that person means by claiming to be born again.

The Presidency and Born Again

Then came Jimmy Carter! Georgia's former governor was relatively unknown on the horizon of national politics. The fact that he claimed to be born again didn't really bother anyone. On the other hand, those who knew what he meant were glad that someone running for president of the United States was born again and not ashamed to say so.

Jimmy Carter's presidential campaign took on new significance when he defeated George Wallace in the Florida Democratic Primary and when he began to win one primary after another. Hubert Humphrey, Ted Kennedy, or one of the candidates opposing Jimmy Carter in the primaries seemed to stand a much better chance of getting the Democratic presidential nomination than did Carter. But when people began to realize that Jimmy Carter just might have a chance of becoming the Democratic nominee for president and that the nominee might become president, his religion took on more importance for both his supporters and his opposition.

Jimmy Carter won the nomination hands down. He then stood an excellent chance of becoming president of the United States. The interest and concern about his religion intensified, and the questions multiplied.

Would Jimmy Carter let his religion affect political decisions? Did a dedicated evangelical belong in the White House? What about this twice-born man's relationship to the once born? Atheists, agnostics, Jews, Catholics, and others had reason to wonder about a born-again person as the chief executive of their government. So the questions came naturally and with feeling.

On the other side of the picture, examples of appreciation for Jimmy Carter's faith came in an Erie, Pennsylvania's voter's words as he shook hands with Carter before the Pennsylvania primary. He told Carter that he, too, was a born-again Christian and that he wanted to express his deep appreciation for Carter's letting his faith in Christ be known. In Americus, Georgia (next door to Plains, Ga., where Carter's home is), a schoolteacher said, "I think the country could use a president who's been born again. I'm for Jimmy Carter."

Regardless of a person's political preferences, it is easy to see that Jimmy Carter's public announcement that he was born again caused more and more people to want to know the meaning of the term. Why? In word and deed he had said and shown that his religion made a difference in his life. He unashamedly wrote about his religion in his autobiography *Why Not the Best?* (Broadman Press: Nashville, Tenn., 1975).

Not since 1960 when John F. Kennedy ran for the presidency had religion really been an issue. But both Kennedy and Carter were open in stating that they believed in separation of church and state. And Billy Graham, who, like Carter, has been born again and is a Southern Baptist, said that just because a political candidate is born again is not reason enough to elect him president. Graham indicated that Gerald Ford also claims to be born again and that religion should not be an issue in the election. But people still wanted to know and want to know what it means to be born again. The question may be real but still be unspoken.

An Unspoken Question

There is evidence that many people who have been born only once would like to know what it means to be born again and how it happens. The silent evidence may speak more loudly than the words of those who voice the questions about being born again.

Suicide dramatically illustrates the desperation of people whose lives come to a dead end and cry out to be born again. When life and its circumstances become unbearable, thousands of people lose hope and choose death rather than continue in their misery. Although they may never have asked what it means to be born again, their death reveals the unspoken question.

However, statistics don't reveal how many people keep on eating, breathing, and vegetating but fail to really live—people who die while they are alive. The stale, purposeless lives cry out for rebirth. They search for happiness in all of the wrong places, and they make gods out of whatever appears to hold any promise of pleasure. And as emotional vagabonds they move on to the next novelty when the last one wears thin and becomes monotonous. Of course, this picture is not accurate for everyone who has been born only once; but the picture does represent countless individuals whose attitudes and actions say, *I want a fresh life;*

I'm tired of my old life. Whether the question is spoken or unspoken, everyone needs to know what it means to be born again.

A Preview of What It Means to Be Born Again

In the seasons of life, a person is born once and experiences childhood, the youth years, adulthood, and death. But that's not the end of life for those who are born again. And that's not all there is to the seasons of life for those who are born again.

In his book *The Seasons of Life,* Dr. Paul Tournier has said that there can be springtimes in autumn! This is what distinguishes man. He recalled an old professor who was born again after he was over eighty years old. The old professor kept saying over and over again, "I'm but a little child; my life has just begun!" Tournier went on to say that the man had become young again, physically as well as emotionally. The experience of being born again penetrates the whole person. [1]

Being born again is not just religious talk; it is a real experience that involves change. People who have lived very long often become skeptical about the thought that anyone can change very much for very long. But people can change. Even adults, who tend to be molded and set in their ways, can choose to make lasting changes in their lives.

People Can Change

Modern students of human behavior are saying what
the Bible has always said: People can change. Thomas
Harris has done an excellent job of making this point
in his book *I'm OK, You're OK* (New York: Harper
and Row, 1969). Since the publication of that book,
many other writers have come up with similar viewpoints and expanded statements of a person's ability to
change. When this viewpoint is set within the Christian context, it means that more than self-will is involved
in the change. More than self-understanding is involved.
God is involved! He enables people to change. The fact
that a person has the ability to choose means that he
can't blame his present and future choices on his parents,
his circumstances, or his culture. The choice of what a
person does with his life is up to him. And in the context of this book, whether a person remains born once
or becomes born again is a choice he has to make. But
he can become a new person.

You're What You're Becoming

A milk commercial used to say that every minute
your body is forming three billion cells and that there
is a new you coming every minute of every day. That
certainly is true in a physical sense, but it is also true
in a spiritual sense about your total being. You're not
what you were; you're what you're becoming.

Strange as it may seem, though, most people do not pay any attention to the truth you've just read. People tend to judge a person and stick with that judgment regardless of how much a person may change. Examples? All right. Read this list of negative terms: conceited, radical, lazy, boring, egotistical, mean, liberal, right-winger, hateful, sadistic, immoral, hypochondriac. Now consider some positive terms: humble, thoughtful, sensitive, interesting, selfless, kind, disciplined, loving, moral, gracious, appreciative, serene. Those are terms you and I have heard used to label persons. We may have used those labels, or they may have been used on us. The point is that once a person is labeled, people seldom think of reexamining the contents and applying new labels.

For another example of unchanging judgment, read what I've repeatedly heard a wife say about her husband: "I can read him like a book." The only problem is that she doesn't read him like a book, for she always recites the same page of his bad points. If she were reading a book, she would go on to see how it all turned out. You see, we often judge a person by only one page of his life. The reason that's so sad is because every person has the possibility of being "The Great Human Novel"—someone and something truly great.

Every person needs to reexamine himself and not sell himself short; he needs to know that he has the grand possibility of being born again. In the shame, disgrace, sadness, disappointment, frustration, and despair of life, each individual would do well to pause and know that every person's *self* is invaluable. What about the errors and weaknesses in life? Well, we don't throw a typewriter away because an error comes from it. We don't throw a Stradivarius violin away or count it worthless just because a sour note comes from it. We recognize the worth and the potential in the typewriter and in the violin. And we can't afford to let our judgment of ourselves or of any other person be determined by individual errors or sour notes that come from his life.

I heard a black preacher quote these words at the beginning of his sermon: "The only man who behaves sensibly toward me is my tailor. For each time we meet he measures me anew, while all the rest continue with their old measurements of me, assuming that they will do. But my tailor measures me anew each time we meet." And at the end of his sermon, the preacher paraphrased: "The only one who behaves sensibly toward me is my Lord. For each time we meet he measures me anew, while all the rest continue with their old measurements of me, assuming that they will do. But my Lord measures me anew each time we meet."

People can change, and people are in the process of becoming. These factors are a preview of what it means to be born again. But there is much more!

2. What the Bible Says

*You have to be born again (Jesus Christ).**

Being born again is not a new term or a new idea. In fact, being born again is so basic to the religious life of millions of people that it is hard to conceive of sophisticated intellectuals not understanding the term. Yet, veteran newswriters are trying to get a little knowledge about the subject in order to explain being born again in people talk (or as the writer to Dear Abby put it: "in easy pool-hall language"). In this case, as in most other cases, a litte knowledge is a deceptive and a dangerous thing.

For example, one writer said that Jimmy Carter's "statements about reborn Christianity are pure fundamentalism, a form of religion that is rising fast in the United States." The writer distorted the term born again that Carter uses and ignored the Christian con-

---

*Author's translation of John 3:7.

text and source of the term. Since the term comes
from a biblical experience, the best place to get the
right answer is the Bible.

It is true that the terms born again and twice born
existed before the Christian New Testament. These
terms were used by Jews to describe non-Jews who
accepted Judaism as their own faith and by those
involved in the ancient Greek religions. However,
the Jews and Greeks did not use the terms in the
same way that Christians speak of being born again
today.

In modern times we talk about getting a new lease
on life or feeling like a new person. But the modern
terms still don't capture the fullness of what a Christian means when he speaks of being born again. So
let's look at the Christian source of the term for the
real meaning.

The Christian Source

The Christian source for the term born again is
Jesus Christ. Jesus told a Jewish leader named Nicodemus, "You have to be born again or you can't have
eternal life" (a summary paraphrase of the interview
between Jesus and Nicodemus). All of this conversa-
tion is recorded in John 3, where Jesus and Nicodemus
used born again eight times in six verses. If you're not
familiar with this passage of Scripture, it will be worth

your time to read the brief interview.

1 There was a man of the Pharisees, named Nicodemus, a ruler of the Jews:

2 The same came to Jesus by night, and said unto him, Rabbi, we know that thou art a teacher come from God: for no man can do these miracles that thou doest, except God be with him.

3 Jesus answered and said unto him, Verily, verily, I say unto thee, Except a man be born again, he cannot see the kingdom of God.

4 Nicodemus saith unto him, How can a man be born when he is old? can he enter the second time into his mother's womb, and be born?

5 Jesus answered, Verily, verily, I say unto thee, Except a man be born of water and of the Spirit, he cannot enter into the kingdom of God.

6 That which is born of the flesh is flesh; and that which is born of the Spirit is spirit.

7 Marvel not that I said unto thee, Ye must be born again.

8 The wind bloweth where it listeth, and thou hearest the sound thereof, but canst not tell whence it cometh, and whither it goeth: so is every one that is born of the Spirit.

9 Nicodemus answered and said unto him, How can these things be?

10 Jesus answered and said unto him, Art thou

a master of Israel, and knowest not these things?

11 Verily, verily, I say unto thee, We speak that we do know, and testify that we have seen; and ye receive not our witness.

12 If I have told you earthly things, and ye believe not, how shall ye believe, if I tell you of heavenly things?

13 And no man hath ascended up to heaven, but he that came down from heaven, even the Son of man which is heaven.

14 And as Moses lifted up the serpent in the wilderness, even so must the Son of man be lifted up:

15 That whosoever believeth in him should not perish, but have eternal life.

16 For God so loved the world, that he gave his only begotten Son, that whosoever believeth in him should not perish, but have everlasting life.

The book of John was originally written in Greek, so the words you've just read from the King James Version of the Bible are a translation of the Greek. There are other English translations of these verses, and there are many interpretations that try to explain the fine points of these verses. For example, "born again" may also be translated "born from above" and "born anew." But the heart of what Jesus taught is not hard to understand. And what Jesus taught is what Christians mean by being born again.

The Heart of the Matter

Nicodemus was a religious leader of the Jews, and he was probably a member of the Jewish "supreme court," the Sanhedrin. But he must have known that there was more to life than what he had experienced. Anyway, he bundled up his admiration and curiosity and came to Jesus. Nicodemus expressed his belief that Jesus had a special relationship with God and had come from God. Perhaps Nicodemus wanted to say more. He may have wanted to compliment Jesus some more and then ask him some questions. But Jesus undoubtedly sensed Nicodemus' unspoken question of how to have life in a different dimension—on a new plane and in a special relationship to God. Then Jesus began to teach Nicodemus.

Jesus used the symbol of birth to teach a spiritual truth. When the literal meaning of words will not do to explain truths that are intense and abstract, we often resort to symbols as a vivid way of expressing what we mean. That's what Jesus did. The Hebrews were familiar with the mystery and the miracle of physical birth. In a time when there were no hospitals and when midwives delivered babies, people would have been keenly aware of the process of physical birth. They knew that husband and wife came together and produced a new creation; and they knew that the new creation came into a world that he had not known before his birth. That's physical birth, and everyone experiences physical birth once.

But being born again? How is that possible? Nicodemus misunderstood Jesus and questioned in a literal way how a person could physically be born again. He knew the answer to his own question. You can't be born again physically. But you can undergo such a radical change that, figuratively speaking, you are born again.

Jesus taught that those who are born again will see the kingdom of God, enter the kingdom of God, and have everlasting life (John 3:3,5,16). The new birth has its beginning and completion in God, but each individual has to choose to be born again; the experience is not automatic.

The Bible teaches that every person chooses his own will instead of God's will. That choice brings God's condemnation and leads to spiritual death (see John 3:18,36). (We'll see why spiritual death is so bad and why everyone needs to be born again when we get to chaps. 4-7.)

The way to eternal life—a new quality of life that is unending—is to openly admit that you have gone against God's will and to openly commit yourself to God's will. Then he can make you a new creation—give you new life and make you born again. God has sent Jesus

Christ to give his life that we may have new life. If we trust Jesus as the gift of God to deliver us from our old stale lives, God gives us new life: life from which there is no dying. *Being born again is a mystery and a miracle that happens in a moment of commitment to Jesus Christ.* The new creation is not born full grown, but he immediately begins to experience life in a new dimension. He realizes that physical death will only open the door to fullness of life in that new dimension. The new dimension is spiritual life.

We'll talk about changes that come in being born again when we get to later chapters. The basic change that we need to focus on now, though, is that a person chooses to let God change his nature by turning himself and all that he has over to God and what he understands God's will to be.

From what little we know about Nicodemus, it seems that he got born again. Later, Nicodemus timidly took a stand that favored Jesus (John 7:45-53). And still later, Nicodemus boldly took part in burying Jesus (John 19:38-39). If Nicodemus was born again, the same God who raised Jesus from the grave to life will also raise Nicodemus (1 Cor. 15). And every person who is born again has the same promise.

We need to emphasize that eternal life—being born again—refers to quality of life and not just length of life. It's one thing to be glad that we can and will have life beyond physical death. But it is good news to know that the quality of life changes at the instant of commitment to Christ. All of our problems are not immediately solved, and we do not instantly become super saints; but we become new creations and begin to live life with a new perspective. We're aware of a new design for our lives and a new source of power as we look to God for guidance.

Life's Supreme Super Moment

Swiss physician-theologian Paul Tournier wrote: "In every life there are a few special moments that count for more than all the rest because they meant the taking of a stand, a self-commitment, a decisive choice. It is commitment that creates the person. It is by commitment that man reveals his humanity."[1] In life we have opportune times that can become life's super moments—the always-remembered moments that go beyond self and time and etch themselves into the granite of eternity. Life's supreme super moment is the moment we are born again through our acceptance of God's gift of Jesus Christ and our commitment to God through following Jesus and turning our lives over to him. That's what the Bible talks about when it talks about being born again. And the Bible has more to say about being born again.

The Bible and Born Again

Although John 3 provides the biblical foundation
for understanding what it means to be born again, you
can't isolate the idea to that one chapter. The Bible
as a whole tells us what it means to be born again. You
can no more isolate the new birth to one chapter of the
Bible than you can isolate the alphabet to one page of
Webster's Third Unabridged Dictionary. The letters
that make up the alphabet appear on all the pages of
the dictionary, and in a similar way we find that what
it means to be born again appears throughout the Bible.
The largeness of the concept is part of the frustration
of even trying to give an overview of what the Bible
has to say about eternal life—life from above. At the
same time, the largeness of the concept is part of the
joy: It is too grand to explain completely in a chapter of a book. Yet, we can continue to focus on special segments of the Bible that reveal more of what it
means to be born again.

Before we look at further Bible passages, let's sum-
marize some biblical thoughts that we need to keep in
mind as we look further: (1) Every person chooses—
consciously or unconsciously—to rebel against God
and his will. (2) The choice is one for spiritual death
instead of spiritual life. (3) God the Creator sent
Jesus, God the Son, to live a perfect life and die on
the cross to deliver mankind from spiritual death and

to spiritual life. (4) Jesus did what God sent him to do, and God raised Jesus from death to live forever. (5) Each person can make a personal commitment to turn his life over to God, be forgiven, and receive the gift of eternal life that Jesus provided. (6) The newborn Christian has the presence and the power of God's Spirit to help him live the new life.

The word picture you've just read may appear to be stained-glass language to you, but perhaps enough light is filtering through so that you're beginning to make out the meaning of what the Bible teaches about being born again. Other Bible passages add even more light.

Romans 6:4 speaks of those who have committed themselves to Christ: "As Christ was raised up from the dead by the glory of the Father, even so we also should walk in newness of life" (KJV). Another word for *newness* is "freshness." There is a freshness to any season of life when we find a new purpose. And God provides that fresh purpose for everyone who turns to him. The experience of new birth enables a person to take his eyes off himself and turn them upon God and his will. The newness comes in the kind of life God has designed for the individual. God's plan for each individual's life is far better than anyone could dream up for himself.

Heaven and hell and life and death are important concerns, but they often ring only of the future. Right now people are tired of monotonous lives that are filled with staleness and purposelessness, and the Bible teaches that those who get born again have a fresh and purposeful life now. I once heard a speaker quote Harry Emerson Fosdick as having said that "life's great moments begin when you meet someone who is perceptive and who realizes the potential in you that has not yet been realized." That someone is God: He will help you experience life's greatest moment in new birth and then a series of great moments in limitless life.

Meeting God is not an accident of life; God is searching for us. A religious organization put on a bright, happy campaign that focused on the theme "I found it!" Outstanding Christians told how they had found Christ and eternal life. They did find Christ and eternal life; but their find was much like a lost child finding the father who was out searching for him. God took the initiative in sending Jesus, and the living Spirit of God continues to urge us to turn his way.

First Peter 1:3 shows that God is behind the new birth: "Blessed be the God and Father of our Lord Jesus Christ! By his great mercy we have been born anew to a living hope through the resurrection of Jesus Christ from the dead" (RSV). And the thought is repeated in 1 Peter 1:23: "You have been born anew, not of perishable seed but of imperishable, through the living and abiding word of God" (RSV). How different this truth is from what the Tibetan poet Milarepa said: "All worldly pursuits end in sorrow,

acquisition in dispersion, buildings in destruction,
meetings in separation, birth in death." For those
who pursue God and his will, just the opposite is
true: Spiritual birth does not end in death but in
life that has no ending and that has a quality the
once born can't conceive of until they become twice
born.

The Bible further teaches that when a person gets
born again it shows up in his life. Though no Christian is perfect, he will not practice rebellion against
God as a way of life: "No one born of God commits sin [makes sin a practice]; for God's nature
abides in him, and he cannot sin [make sin a prac-
tice] because he is born of God" (1 John 3:9, RSV;
brackets are the author's translation). Some people
appear to get religion and then lose it overnight,
and only God can judge who really gets his nature
changed in an experience of commitment. But,
as an old saying has it, when a person gets religion,
it's not how high he jumps that counts; it's how
straight he walks when he comes down.

The Bible says that love for others is another sign
that a person has been born again: "Beloved, let us
love one another; for love is of God, and he who
loves is born of God and knows God" (1 John 4:7).
Some people try to define love by dividing it into
various expressions. But there's nothing difficult
about understanding the kind of love that is spoken

of here: It is an active concern that is willing to sacrifice—a love like God's love. The life that lacks this love lacks one of the evidences of spiritual life.

When the newborn Christian does wrong or fails to show God's kind of love, he may feel that he is still only once born and that he does not have eternal life. And feelings are hard to deal with. But another sign of spiritual life is taking God at his word—believing God. And God's Word says, "We know that any one born of God does not sin [make sin a practice], but He who was born of God keeps him, and the evil one does not touch him" (1 John 5:18, RSV; brackets are the author's translation). You will remember that Jesus was referred to as the only begotten Son of God (John 3:16). *He is the one born of God* who protects and sustains the rest of us who have been born again. Eternal life depends on the experience of commitment to God through Jesus and not on our feelings. And we can no more become unborn spiritually than we can become unborn physically. This is what the Bible teaches. Faith in God's promise is more important than the human feelings that change with the circumstances of life.

The Bible points people to God and to new life. Gideons International tries to place Bibles wherever people are. And the Gideons have volumes of letters that tell how people have reached personal decisions to turn from the way they are living and

thinking and to turn to God. Those letters usually
tell how the individuals picked up a Gideon Bible,
read it, realized their condition, and followed the
directions of the Bible in getting born again. People
can learn what it means to be born again by reading
the Bible. Of course, there are those who refuse to
believe the Bible. Every person has the right to believe or not to believe; however, those who do not
believe tend to be those who do not read and study
the Bible. The Bible is the book to read. Some of
the greatest intellectual giants of the world are among
those who have read the Bible, believed it, and acted
upon its truths.

The Bible and Other Books

Although the Bible doesn't need a defense, it is good
to know that it can stand up under the most penetrat-
ing criticism. Some people say, "The Bible says it; I
believe it; and that settles it"; and they smile with
pride. That approach is all right for those who can
accept it, for the Bible is true; and believing objective
truth is more important than knowing why you believe it.

What about people who question the Bible and want
proof about this business of being born again? Is there
no help for those who read the Bible and doubt what
they read? Yes, there is help. Dr. Elton Trueblood has

written *A Place to Stand.* The book begins with the belief that Christianity is reasonable; and it moves on to other chapters that reinforce the concept. The book is filled with thoughts and experiences such as this one:

"In the face of the abundant evidence of prayer it is hard to dogmatize. About all the skeptic can do is to reply that, though the result prayed for does sometimes occur, this is a mere coincidence. The solemnity of this confident answer was in one instance somewhat shaken by the humor of William Temple, when he admitted that it was conceivable that the events which occurred in his wonderful and productive life were merely coincidental, but added that the coincidences came more frequently when he prayed."[2]

Dr. Trueblood's explanation of the Christian faith and of the Bible as truth is not that of a naive person. Dr. Trueblood admitted that he came from skepticism to belief in the matter of Christ's resurrection from the grave. Trueblood himself admired the late C. S. Lewis, who took the long way through various intellectual pursuits to become *Surprised by Joy* (London: Geoffrey Bles, 1955). Lewis learned that God is real, that eternal life comes in accepting Christ as Master and Savior, and that the Bible was right all the time.

Trueblood and Lewis are only two skeptics who came to believe Bible truths that provide insights into being born again. Yet their lives—and the lives of many others like them—show that there is room for the person who has doubts. The Bible is the book to read, but there are other books that shed light on the Bible.

The Bottom Line

We live in an impatient world, where people often want the speaker or writer to get to the bottom line— and in a hurry. The bottom line of what the Bible says about eternal life is this: You have to be born again. The decision is an individual one. This fact underlies the following chapters of this book. Nicodemus had a personal choice to make, and so does everyone else. To remain undecided is to decide against Christ and the life he offers. To decide that you don't need to be born again is to decide to ignore the basic teaching of the Bible. To reason away the need to be born again is unreasonable. To have new life you have to turn your life over to God; then he can give you the gift of eternal life. And your life will never be the same again.

3. From the Bible to Now

*The church is most faithful to its tradition,
and realizes its unity with the church of
every age, when linked but not tied by its
past, it today searches the Scriptures and
orients its life by them as though this had
to happen today for the first time (Karl Barth).*

To people who don't know much biblical or religious history, the idea of being born again may sound like a fad or a new idea. But the term is as old as the New Testament, and the thought is even older than that.

We have overviewed the biblical teachings of the New Testament about the meaning of the new birth, and that brought us roughly up to A.D. 100. From the Bible to now, though, people have gotten a lot of different ideas about what it means to be born again. Some of the ideas are right; some are wrong; and many people are confused about what to believe.

This chapter will deal with some of the departures from the biblical teachings and how they came about.

It will also try to reinforce what the Bible teaches
about the new birth. This approach should help us
get a better view of the present uncertainty about
what it means to be born again.

How the Church Grew and Changed

People are free to believe as they want to, and various individuals and groups have chosen to hold beliefs
that are hard to square with what the Bible teaches.
Of course, those who haven't read the Bible don't
really know what it teaches and couldn't be expected
to square their views with those of the Bible. However,
people who do read the Bible and look to it for their
understanding of eternal life often differ in their viewpoints. Frank S. Mead's *Handbook of Denominations
in the United States* (Nashville: Abingdon Press, 1970)
lists over 250 religious bodies just within the United
States. So a brief look at how the church grew and
changed will give some insight into why all churches
don't agree in their emphasis and understanding of how
a person becomes a Christian and receives eternal life.

Jesus founded the church (see Matt. 16:18). The
word *church* basically refers to a summoned assembly.
And within the context of the New Testament, the
church was made up of the followers of Jesus. In a
spiritual sense, Jesus is the head of the church, which
is made up of all of his followers (see Eph. 5:23; Col.

1:18). However, most of the references in the New
Testament are to specific churches in specific cities.
In those early churches, some of the Jewish Christians
believed that converts to Christianity also had to become converts to Judaism to become born again (see
Gal. 5; Acts 15). This controversy led to a restatement
of the truth that people are born again only by putting
their trust in Jesus Christ as their Lord and Savior. *The
churches of the New Testament agreed on what it took
to be born again.* Churches today do not all agree on
what is necessary. What happened between then and
now? The church grew and changed.

The development of the church and of Christendom
from A.D. 100 to now is an interesting story. If you're
interested in reading one book that paints a panoramic
view, you could do no better than to read Robert
Baker's *A Summary of Christian History* (Nashville:
Broadman Press, 1959). From his book we can get
some summary thoughts that will help us.

From roughly the time of Christ's crucifixion to
about A.D. 300, the Roman government persecuted
the Christians. The persecuted Christians dispersed
and took their New Testament teachings with them.
They defended their faith, told about the certainty
of their hope, and pointed people to Jesus Christ as
the source of salvation.

The Christians witnessed to others about what had
happened in their lives, and the end result was often

suffering or death. Polycarp was the student of John
the apostle, and Polycarp was put to death about the
middle of the second century A.D. In a letter titled
Martyrdom of Polycarp, we read the following testi-
mony:

"The Proconsul urged him and said, 'Swear, and I
will release thee; curse the Christ.' And Polycarp said,
'Eighty and six years have I served him, and he hath
done me no wrong; how then can I blaspheme my
king who saved me?' " [1] The focus was on Christ as
Savior.

In A.D. 250 Bishop Cyprian said, "No man can have
God for his Father who does not have the Church for
his mother." About that same time Cyprian said,
"Where the bishop is, there is the church, and there
is no church where there is no bishop." Robert Baker
wrote, "By 325 faith had lost its personal character as
being the whole dependence of a person immediately
upon the person and work of Jesus Christ. Rather,
while Christ was a part of the system, faith was to be
directed toward the institution called the Church; and
salvation did not result from the immediate regenerating
power of the Holy Spirit but was mediated by the sacraments of baptism and the Lord's Supper."[2]

What had happened? Constantine the Great came
on the scene and exchanged imperial persecution of the
church with toleration and then with favor. At first he
would not persecute the Christians as they had been

persecuted in the past (about A.D. 305). In A.D. 311 he issued an edict that called for toleration of Christians. In A.D. 325 he issued a general plea for his subjects to become Christians. And between A.D. 378-95, under Theodosius, Christianity became the official state religion. Scholars have commented that Christianity has never quite recovered from the exchange of imperial favor for imperial persecution. The reasons behind that statement are complex, and you need to trace the full development. But we can look at some of the changes in a nutshell.

Although some individual religious leaders had become more powerful and some degree of hierarchy was in existence before Constantine, he added to the elements that were taking churches away from the New Testament pattern. Under Constantine's influence masses of people came into the church without ever being born again. They were counterfeit or misguided Christians, and they brought their paganism and impurities with them. The way to salvation was perverted to focus on belonging to an institution instead of hearing the institution's message about Christ and responding to him. This development should help anyone see that although Christians wear their name because they are supposed to be followers of Christ, no one should judge Christ by his followers alone: They may be counterfeit Christians, those who may wear the name Christian without having been born again.

Some Unbiblical Ideas

As someone has remarked, Christianity came from the catacombs of Rome to the throne in less than a century. But on its journey to the throne, several unbiblical ideas grew stronger. It was taught that baptism was necessary for salvation. Grace (God's favor) became something that a person received through the church rather than directly from God. The congregations that had earlier looked to God and tried to rule themselves by his will were now looking to powerful bishops for directives. And eventually they looked to Rome as the head of the church. We can speak of the period of papal development as being from A.D. 325–1215; and the period of Western reform was from A.D. 1215–1648. It was in 1302 that Pope Boniface VIII stated that *outside the church there is no salvation.*

In many ways, this was the dark age of the church. But careful study through the years of darkness shows that there were always rays of light shining through and telling us what it meant to be born again. The Scriptures that were so sadly neglected were preserved for a time when people would once again see the need to square their beliefs and actions with Bible teachings.

Unless you are a student of history, you would not believe all that has gone on in the name of religion—and particularly between A.D. 325–1517. Religious leaders taught doctrine that had no scriptural basis, became involved in gross immorality as a way of life, set themselves above the head of their government, and treated Christlike people as heretics to be strangled and burned. *Not all religious leaders were like this, but many were.* The Roman Catholic Church was the state church, and at times there was really no separation of church and state. People learned and believed ridiculous ideas about salvation. For salvation the people looked to the institutional church, sacraments (baptism, the Lord's Supper, and others), and works. There was a lack of emphasis on salvation as a gift of God to be received through trusting Jesus Christ.

To balance this black picture with the rays of light mentioned earlier, read *Forward Through the Ages* by Basil Mathews (New York: Friendship Press, 1960). This book shows that there were concerned people who were trying to do the will of God during the years of darkness. This contrast of behavior points out even more vividly the responsibility of each individual to God and his fellowman, regardless of what others may do.

New Beginnings

The end of the long night of spiritual darkness came with the dawning of new beginnings. The thirteenth and fourteenth centuries were like the dim light of a new day that burst into a spiritual sunrise during the sixteenth century.

The Bible had been available primarily in Hebrew, Greek, and Latin for the educated few who could read these languages. Wycliffe, Tyndale, and Coverdale were men who gave themselves to translating the Bible into English so the common people of England could read the Bible for themselves. Martin Luther translated the Bible into German. The printing press was invented. And people were alive with a spiritual hunger that was not being met.

Martin Luther was the spark who ignited the Reformation. He was about twenty-two when a bolt of lightning struck nearby and scared him out of his wits. He had already had some feelings that he needed to get right with God, and that event convinced him. He entered a monastery, and he didn't find spiritual peace there. He did good works; he confessed sins he could remember and those he couldn't remember; and he studied and taught the Bible. What he learned from the Bible led him to new life and peace. He realized that new life was possible only by forsaking anything that stood in the way and by trusting Christ. With his new biblical insights, he wanted the church to reform and return to biblical teachings about salvation and many other things. On October 31, 1517 he nailed up a list of ninety-five theses or points he wanted to debate. That was in the day when you could be burned for disagreeing with the state church.

In a debate before the religious leaders that could

have ended in his death, Martin Luther concluded by stating: "Unless I am convicted by Scripture and plain reason—I do not accept the authority of popes and councils, for they have contradicted each other— my conscience is captive to the Word of God. I cannot and I will not recant anything, for to go against conscience is neither right nor safe. God help me. Amen." And the earliest printed version added what he undoubtedly thought, even if he did not voice it: "Here I stand, I cannot do otherwise." [3]

Surprisingly enough, Luther lived to die of old age; but even if he hadn't, he was born again, and all death could do would be to open the door to a fuller life.

Along with Luther came Zwingli, Calvin, the Anabaptists, and other reformers. They differed in understanding various parts of the Bible, and they differed in their views on church government, the Lord's Supper, baptism, pacifism, and other matters. But they agreed in essence on what it takes to be born again. The Protestant Reformation changed the complexion of the religious scene in the sixteenth and following centuries. The word *protest* meant more than raise an objection; it meant to speak in behalf of. Those who joined in protesting felt they were confessing and reaffirming the pattern of faith found in the early New Testament churches.

Since the Protestant Reformation, there have been reformations within the Roman Catholic Church, all

sorts of groups of evangelicals who are free from being
a state church, and splinter sects. There have been
great awakenings after periods of spiritual droughts.
We don't have the space to trace even the major
thrusts of religious developments since the Reformation. But we can safely say that the Reformation put
individual faith and the collective expression of that
faith back into perspective and provided a better balance.

The church is important. Jesus purchased the church—
the born-again people—with his own blood (see Acts
20:28). However, the church doesn't save anyone. It
has the responsibility of sharing the message of salvation. And this perspective is what came back into focus
for multitudes during the period of the Protestant
Reformation. At the same time, we would have to
recognize that many people did not change in their
perspective then or now: They still believe that salvation comes through the church and its sacraments.
They are free to believe as they will, but they would
do well to come back to the point of reference.

Point of Reference

An investigation of the crash of a jet plane took over
a year to complete. When the study was over and the
results were in, the verdict was that the crash came because of pilot error—error on the part of an experienced,
well-trained pilot. It seems that the pilot saw some

groundlights that became his point of reference. But the lights were in a steep valley, and the plane crashed because the pilot didn't look at his altimeter to check the altitude until it was too late to pull the plane up from the ground.

You see, point of reference can mean the difference between life and death. Many people ignore the Bible as their point of reference and still can't understand why their lives are in a tailspin and why they are headed for a crash.

A young pastor told his congregation, "We are a generation of biblical illiterates who can read, a generation who believe the Bible but don't know what it says." He drew his conclusion from looking at the lives people live, listening to their convictions, and testing their Bible knowledge. When people do not live right, do not speak right, and do not think right, you have to wonder about their point of reference.

People sometimes think they are living right when they are actually upside down. Without a point of reference, you can't tell whether you're right side up or upside down. After some astronauts had gone to the moon and back, they were viewing films of the command ship and the lunar module that had separated in space. One of the astronauts commented to another one, "You're upside down." The reply came, *"Someone* was upside down." They were joking, but they proved the point: A point of reference is essential if we're to know whether we're right side up.

You can't even spell correctly without a point of reference, and even then you have to choose your point of reference. For example, look up the word *pizzazz* in a half dozen dictionaries that came out in the seventies. You'll find several different spellings. You have to choose which dictionary will serve as your point of reference.

How can a person expect to live an orderly life with meaning and not have the right point of reference? If the morals of our time and the changing beliefs of our generation are your point of reference, then you have chosen to ignore the Bible as your point of reference. If the Bible is your point of reference, you have guidance about how God wants you to live. Although no one is perfect, the Bible helps set the standard for judging life and for knowing which direction to turn. Conscience is not a reliable guide unless conscience is beamed in on the Word of God. You can't go by your senses alone. You have to tie your conscience and your senses to the Word of God. In that Word you will find Jesus, and he will give you a new life. You won't quit being human, but you will share in eternal life and will receive a new nature that lets you live in a spiritual dimension that you never lived in before.

The Protestant Reformation returned to the point of reference believed and written by first-century

Christians. The reformers put Scripture above tradition, but they did not totally reject tradition.

Tradition Has Its Place

Tradition can be helpful in interpreting Scripture. The person who looks at the attempts of those who have gone before him to interpret Scripture will be able to see alternative viewpoints and to avoid many mistakes of the past. We can't afford to reject the wisdom of the past, but neither can we afford to let tradition preempt the primary place of the Bible as the source for Christian teaching.

Perhaps some examples will give us better insight to the proper role of tradition. In the movie *Fiddler on the Roof,* Tevye, the main character, said, "How do we keep our balance? Tradition! Because of our tradition, we've kept our balance for many, many years. Because of our tradition, every one of us knows who he is and what God expects him to do. Without our tradition, our lives would be as shaky as a fiddler on the roof."

Tradition gives us some guidance to travel by. Not long ago the road I commute on was resurfaced, and there were no lines to indicate the lanes for quite some time. I watched people wander all over the narrow road and saw that the number of accidents increased significantly. People needed some lines to guide them.

When the lines got painted, people began to do a better job of driving in a straight line and of not getting in each other's way. Tradition does something like this for us—especially when tradition has the Bible for its point of reference.

Neither tradition nor the Bible is to be worshiped. But each has its place. Tradition points us to man and his attempts to understand God and his will. The Bible points us to Jesus (John 5:39-40, RSV), and he is the one who supremely interprets God and his will and provides us with eternal life if we will trust our lives to him.

Believing the Bible is not a matter of blind faith or of following naive traditions. Some of the wisest philosophical and scientific minds of our era have concluded that the truths of the Bible are the wisest choices from all those that are possible. In the study of knowledge, the last step of proof is always a leap of faith. People who have tested the alternatives and have been born again know by experience that the best leap of faith is toward the Bible and Jesus as the one the Bible reveals. And as someone has said, "The person who has had an experience is never at the mercy of the one who merely has an argument." (For further explanation, read Elton Trueblood's *A Place to Stand.*)

Truths Rediscovered

The Protestant reformers discovered some old truths

that led them to bring much of their tradition in line with the teachings of the Bible. We can't look at all of those rediscovered truths, but let's look at a few of the main truths.

They discovered the place of the Bible and that the Bible is to be interpreted by the standard of Jesus Christ. They rediscovered that new birth comes by committing oneself individually to Jesus and receiving salvation as a gift—not something to be bought or worked for. They discovered all over again that a person can be certain about his salvation.

The Anabaptists (rebaptizers) taught believer's baptism. In other words, they recognized that baptism is for adults and that baptism doesn't have any saving power in itself. It is a symbol that pictures dying to an old way of life and thought and being raised to a new way of life and thought. They came to see that water sprinkled or poured on infants had no power because infants were not old enough to be believers.

The reformers rediscovered that a person doesn't have to go through a priest to talk to God and to receive God's blessings. This doctrine is called the *priesthood of the believer.* It means that each person can be his own priest and pray directly to God. This teaching does not in any way take away from the need for teachers, preachers, and other religious leaders; but it does put those positions in proper perspective.

A person is not born again because of getting sprinkled
or having the blessing of a priest. He is not born again because he is confirmed into adult privileges of church mem-
bership when he reaches a certain age. A person is not born
again simply by being born into a Christian family and by
attending their church with them. A person is born again
when he recognizes his rebellion against God and makes
the individual decision to trust Jesus Christ and become
a follower of his. No matter what religious label a person
may wear, if he makes the decision to trust Jesus as Lord
and Savior, the person begins a new life that never ends.
It is a life of higher quality than he ever could have
imagined before he had the experience. Whether a person is a Methodist, a Baptist, an Episcopalian, a Roman
Catholic, or a member of some other group, if he is born
again, he has the experience the same way: by trusting
Jesus as Lord and Savior. This is what the apostles knew.
It is what Martin Luther discovered. And it is what
believers of every age have known. Trusting Christ is
an experience that is not confined to a region, a race,
or an age of history.

The Protestant Reformation roughly dates from
1517, when Luther tacked his ninety-five theses up
for debate, to 1648, when the Peace of Westphalia
marked the end to thirty years of war. That period of
rediscovery was a period of new beginnings that continue
even today. We've gone through periods of extreme paganism and puritanism; we've gone through great awakenin

of spiritual revivals, and we've come through some severe spiritual droughts. But perhaps we have learned some lessons that will keep us from making mistakes made in the past.

As we read earlier, Karl Barth said: "The church is most faithful to its tradition, and realizes its unity with the church of every age, when linked but not tied by its past, it today searches the Scriptures and orients its life by them as though this had to happen today for the first time." [4] So, to conclude this chapter, let's be sure we know what the Bible teaches about being born again.

Once More from the Bible

The Bible teaches that rebirth is an individual experience that occurs when a person turns from self-commitment and commits himself to trust and follow Jesus Christ as the Master of his life.

Christ is God the Son. He always was, always is, and always will be. There never was a time when Christ did not exist. But in a moment of time he became a human being. He followed God the Father's plan that existed before the foundation of the world. Born of a virgin, Jesus lived a sinless life and then voluntarily died on the cross to provide forgiveness for the sins of all mankind and to provide eternal life. He died on the cross and lay buried in the tomb for part of three days; then God raised him to live forevermore.

Individuals who knew Christ and saw him dead also saw him resurrected and alive. Literally hundreds of people saw Jesus alive after his death.

The whole sequence of birth, life, death, and resurrection is sometimes called the Christ Event. And all who will become Christians—who will become born again—have the same promise of eternal life that Jesus has. The gift of eternal life is God's gift of grace, which means that God has given mankind a gift man did not and could not deserve. Accepting the gift is *the* way of accepting new life, a new nature.

Although the whole Bible opens the door to God's will and his provision for eternal life, John 3 and 1 Corinthians 15 are two chapters of the Bible that most clearly tell what the Bible means when it speaks of being born again. These truths are foundational for further study and understanding. Still, the few words you have read barely shed light on the quality of life and the fullness of life involved in being born again. There is much more, but the primary reason we have looked at the Bible once more is to focus on the individual decision of commitment to Christ. That fact is the essence of rebirth.

Traditional religious terminology would use some of the language I have used, but it would also speak of conviction of sin, repentance of sin, confession of sin, believing on Jesus as Lord and Savior. I have tried to explain some of the traditional terminology, and

I've tried to use everyday language that calls for less explanation. But whatever the terminology, we may best be able to see what it means to be born again by seeing the changes that come about in the experience. We can tell about the changes, and we can see the changes illustrated in the lives of individuals. So in explaining what it means to be born again, the next focus will be on change.

4. Changes That Take Place

The butterfly is nature's most visible illustration of rebirth. Once drab and earthbound as a caterpillar, the butterfly emerges from its cocoon in beautifully radiant colors, soaring upward into the sky. Free—BORN AGAIN— just as each of us can be when we are, through Christ, born again in the Spirit (Charles Colson). [1]

Charles Colson's illustration is a good one. He experienced a change in his own life that was as drastic as that of a caterpillar becoming a butterfly. Years before Colson had his experience, Dr. Harry Rimmer used the same illustration to describe the new birth. He wrote a booklet titled *Flying Worms,* and in that booklet he said: "When the early biologists found out that caterpillars changed into butterflies and could not discover how, they wanted to describe the process. So they took the old Greek word *metamorphomai* and made it into the modern form of 'metamorphosis' which we still use to describe the birth of a butterfly!

"So you see our parable is very exact—we do become 'changed' by the inexplicable mystery and wonder of the New Birth, just as worms get wings by a process of metamorphosis." [2] *Metamorphosis* is a big word, but it is a good one to describe the drastic change in form or state of existence that occurs in various areas of life. *The Oxford English Dictionary* describes metamorphosis in relationship to persons as a "complete change in the appearance, circumstances, condition, character of a person." We see the thought of that description as we look at Matthew 17:1-2, Romans 12:1-2, and 2 Corinthians 3:18.

MATTHEW 17:1-2

1 And after six days Jesus taketh Peter, James, and John his brother, and bringeth them up into an high mountain apart,

2 And was transfigured before them: and his face did shine as the sun, and his raiment was white as the light.

ROMANS 12:1-2

1 I beseech you therefore, brethren, by the mercies of God, that ye present your bodies a living sacrifice, holy, acceptable unto God, which is your reasonable service.

2 And be not conformed to this world: but be ye transformed by the renewing of your mind, that ye may prove what is that good, and acceptable, and perfect, will of God.

2 CORINTHIANS 3:18

18 But we all, with open face beholding as in a glass the glory of the Lord, are changed into the same image from glory to glory, even as by the Spirit of the Lord.

In all three of these Bible passages from the King James Version, the Greek verb for metamorphosis is used; and the English translation comes in this order: *transfigured, transformed, changed* (following the order of the Scriptures listed). In the new birth we do not quit being human beings, but we become new beings—new spiritual beings. The person who experiences the change may not be able to explain it any better than he can tell how and why a caterpillar is able to become a butterfly, but he knows that he is a transformed person and that he will never be the same again. The reborn person has the same shell for a body, but he is a new person in commitment, thinking, direction, relationships, and in many other ways.

Change, in general, is not necessarily good; but the change that occurs in the new birth is always good. It is the best thing that could ever happen to a person. So let's look at a person's condition before the new birth and then see what happens in and after the new birth.

Before the New Birth

Everybody is born once. Not everybody is born
twice. But there comes a time in the life of every person when he needs to be born again. (This need may
be part of the hardest thing to understand in explaining what it means to be born again.) Each person
reaches a stage and a time in life when he chooses
his own will instead of what God wills. What is so
bad about that? The Bible speaks of that choice as sin
that results in spiritual death: a separation from God
and a basic nature that is sinful. The only way out of
that spiritual death is through the experience of spiritual birth.

Sin is described as missing the mark; and if you picture a target and an archer or marksman, you begin
to get the picture of one who has missed the target.
But the picture of sin is a little different from that.
People miss the mark of God's will because they do
not aim at the target; they turn their back on the target, and they choose their own direction. In the evil
of life we see the expressions of what sin is now and
why a person needs to be born again. God always
wants what is best for people. But when they choose
their design for living instead of his design, we see
life at its worst (and certainly at less than its best):
murder, adultery, alcoholism, crime, hatred, jealousy,
war, selfishness, insecurity, lying, pride, self-righteous-

ness, and an almost endless list of things that obviously
are wrong and bad. When people are involved in these
kinds of activities or attitudes, they reveal a need to be
born again.

However, many people are decent, law-abiding citizens who are not involved in any of the things listed.
Why do they need to be born again? The Bible teaches
that negative goodness doesn't exempt a person from
the need to be born again. In other words, a person is
not good just because he avoids doing the bad things
of life. The person who does not commit himself to
Jesus Christ and does not commit his life and posses-
sions to the service of God is also a sinner in need of
being born again. Read Matthew 25:14-30. The one
person described as being wicked was the one who did
nothing good with what he had. Good deeds never
made anyone a Christian, but they do reflect something about a person's commitment to Christ. The
failure to trust Christ as Lord and Savior is sin, and
that failure shows up in how a person spends his time,
his money, and his energies. Everyone chooses his will
over God's will and enters into spiritual death; consequently, everyone needs to be born again. This is the
teaching of the Bible.

No matter how good a person's life appears to be
without Christ, it will be infinitely better with Christ.
And the same is true for nations. Before a person is
born again, he doesn't realize his potential or the quality

of life available to him; but God realizes that and takes
the initiative in appealing to everyone to commit himself to follow Christ and be born again.

After the New Birth

We have tried to look at the new birth from a variety
of perspectives, and we'll continue to do that to show
the many-splendored facets of life's supreme experience.
We have seen that people from all walks of life are asking what it means to be born again. We have seen that
people are confused and have different viewpoints
about what it means to be born again. This problem
is nothing new; it has existed from the Bible to now.
One thing is for sure: Born-again people say that a
drastic change takes place in the experience of new
birth. We'll come back and look at the moment of new
birth and those factors surrounding that moment, but
right now we'll contrast the changes of condition that
occur after the new birth.

Theologian William L. Hendricks has given us one of
the clearest pictures of the *before* and *after* of salvation
in a sermon titled "Full Salvation" (see *Southwestern
Sermons,* compiled by H. C. Brown, Nashville: Broadman Press, 1960, pp. 122-128). In his sermon, Hendricks
did not shy away from religious language; rather, he
pointed out the need to explain the language. He freely
used *salvation* to tell about the new birth. People who

use the language of the Bible and of the church often
speak of being saved. In fact, Christians who are concerned about the condition of others and want to
share the good news Christ offers may ask, "Are you
saved?" The question offends some, brings knowing
smiles from others, and draws a wide variety of answers
from those who take the question seriously.

Are you saved? Here are some of the answers I've
heard to that question: I hope so. I used to be, but
the church burned down. I don't think so. It doesn't
matter what you believe as long as you are sincere.
We are all trying to get to the same place. If my mother
was a Christian, I am. I'll be there one of these days.
I'm no saint, but I live a lot better life than some church
members. I've lived too bad a life to be saved. When
I'm ready to become a Christian, I'm going to live it.
I used to be a Christian, but I haven't been to church
in a long time.

These answers to life's crucial question have come
from ordinary people. They have associated salvation
with being good, getting better, and going to church.
The *association* is natural and right, but it does not
get to the heart of what happens when a person gets
saved. Hendricks explained that salvation is through
an experience with Jesus Christ. It happens and
doesn't *unhappen.* He explained the root meaning of
salvation and that salvation is both *from* something
and *to* something.

In the Old Testament the word for *salvation* originally meant wide, spacious, developing without hin-
drance. It came to mean deliverance from trouble.
In a troubled, tangled world that tends to crush people into what they were not meant to be, we can appreciate the possibilities involved in salvation. Other
Old Testament words that relate to salvation are deliverance, victory, wealth, happiness, prosperity, and
peace. Aside from religious interest, people would
seemingly have a natural interest in an experience
that could have those elements in it.

The New Testament verb for *save* is from a root
word meaning to restore to health or to rescue from
danger. We're interested in that meaning also, aren't
we?

For some people, salvation is a well-preserved experience from the past that they consider essential
to the future but one that does not vitally affect the
present. Because of the biblical meanings of salvation, we can see that salvation refers to all of life;
and salvation comes in the new birth. One emphasis
that we need to focus on over and over again is that
no one can save himself. God does the saving, but
man does the responding to the offer of salvation
(see Ps. 3:8; Eph. 2:8-10). And we need to realize
that salvation is not something that refers just to
that part of us we may think of as the soul. When
the Hebrews thought of the soul, they thought of

the whole person. Salvation is for all of life: physical, mental, emotional, spiritual.

Salvation is from something and to something. Unashamedly, we admit that salvation is from hell and to heaven (see Luke 3:7; John 3; Rom. 6:23; Rev. 21:6-8). Some interpret the picture of hell literally, and others interpret the picture figuratively. The literal picture is horrible; and if the wording is to be taken figuratively, we have seen that symbolic language often portrays things that are too intense to put into literal words.

Hell is not something you hear preached on much in a lot of quarters today, and some of the preaching on the subject may not be what it ought to be. Nevertheless, to be delivered from unending existence in hell to the unending joy of heaven is a real reason for considering the new birth. This change in a person's spiritual status is staggering in its importance. (You can study more about hell by turning to Matt. 3:12; 8:12; 22:13; 25:30; Mark 9:44, 48; and Rev. 14:10; 20:14.) God is everywhere, but heaven especially speaks of where God is; and it is where Christians will eventually be (see Matt. 5:12; 24:36; Luke 15:18; Rev. 18:20).

Much of the hell that people face is not just in the future; it is now. So many of us could say about the problems of life, "I have met the enemy, and he is me." We are saved from self (Rom. 7:24 to 8:1). No one is born full grown, but the Christian has God to help him grow and overcome the self that does wrong.

We're saved from sin (Matt. 1:21). Because we're still human, we don't quit sinning (1 John 1:8). But we quit practicing sin as a way of life (1 John 3:6-9). From the new birth on we have a new nature that points us in a new direction. We may miss the target of God's will; but after the new birth we're facing the target, and there are evidences that we are aiming at the target—no matter how far short we may fall. The Christian is able to start pleasing God (see Rom. 8:6-9).

The Christian is reconciled to God (see 2 Cor. 5:17-20; Eph. 2:14-17). God has not turned his back on the person who is not a Christian; it is the other way around. And that turning away from God came through a personal choice to sin—to rebel against God. We're used to hearing the term *reconciliation* in the context of marriage. In most cases onlookers will admit that both a husband and wife are partly at fault in a separation or divorce; and when reconciliation takes place, they have both overlooked some faults and come back to a peaceful relationship. But in the case of God and man, God is not the one who needs to be reconciled; it is man, for man alone has done the sinning. In the new birth experience, God forgives the offender, and the offender is reconciled to God. This great change does away with a lot of the inner war that a person has in himself before the new birth, and it puts him at peace with God.

After the new birth, we have a new promise and a
new power to overcome the temptations and the troubles
that come our way in life (see 1 Cor. 10:13; 2 Cor. 12:9).
In this nerve-racking world, almost everyone seems to be
looking for a sedative that will tranquilize him; but God
promises the Christian a challenge that puts energy to
work and gives an inner peace that passes human understanding. This is something of what it means to be saved
to eternal life and fellowship with God (1 John 1:7).
God provides the new birth through Jesus Christ and an
individual's response to Jesus. So a person is not saved
by good deeds, but he certainly is saved to work with
God in doing them (Eph. 2:10). Salvation does affect
all of life.

Recently I heard a pastor tell of visiting in the home
of a man whose life had more of hell in it than of heaven.
The man had problems in just about every area of life.
He had been in the military and was wounded and no
longer a whole man in a physical sense—and certainly
not in an emotional sense. His family had left him. The
pastor heard the man say, "What I need is to be made
over again." And the pastor was able to tell him, "The
good news is that you can be made over again; you can
be born again."

People Can Change

What you've been reading about in religious terms is

something that people are talking about in psychological terms. They may have different goals in mind, but they have come to recognize that people can change. Of course, the Christian perspective is that God initiates, sustains, and completes the new birth. But individuals have to respond to God. Still, whether in the realm of religion or in the realm of psychology, people have become aware that people can change.

In *I'm OK, You're OK,* Thomas Harris wrote: "Transactional Analysis . . . has given a new answer to people who want to change rather than to adjust, to people who want transformation rather than conformation [see Rom. 12:1-2]. It is realistic in that it confronts the patient with the fact that he is responsible for what happens in the future no matter what has happened in the past. Moreover, it is enabling persons to change, to establish self-control and self-direction, and to discover the reality of a freedom of choice."

Further, Harris wrote: "It is a profoundly rewarding experience to see people begin to change from the first treatment hour, get well, grow, and move out of the tyranny of the past . . . . If individuals can change, the course of the world can change. This is a hope worth sustaining." [3]

In *The Seasons of Life* Paul Tournier wrote, "In the light both of the Bible and of modern science, then, we are confronted not with an abstract and

generalized man, but with men who are concrete and
personal. They are always *in their context,* in a certain relationship to the world, to others, and to God.
They are always changing." Tournier added, "Life is
not a harmless diversion or a chance adventure; it is
the crucial game which we can play only once. This
game must of necessity end in victory or defeat."
And for the person who thinks life is hopeless and he
personally is beyond change, Tournier would give him
reason to take heart: "At every moment, no matter
what the accumulated ruins may be, there is a plan
of God to be found." [4]

The Bible has taught for hundreds and thousands
of years that people can change. People can do more
than change as a natural consequence of time; they
can commit themselves to God in a way that changes
their condition for all time and eternity. In that personal surrender to God and his will, a person doesn't
lose his individuality or choice; but he moves to a
higher level of *becoming.* He takes the step that
opens the door to his becoming all that he has the
potential to become. In *The Becomers* Keith Miller
wrote, "Regardless of the circumstances surrounding
a person's surrender, and whatever the specific 'content' of his experience, there almost always follows a
strange awareness that he has entered a whole new
segment of his life—as if he had turned a page and begun a new chapter. Jesus said this fresh vision of life

is life being 'born again' (John 3:3). The recently converted Christian has a whole new cluster of motivating
needs. He wants to become different from his past.
And what this seems to mean in practical terms is that
he is highly motivated to learn a whole new style of
living . . . . His old dominant values and the frantic
sense of responsibility for his own success don't seem
important as compared to learning about God and his
will in ordinary life. And whether the convert's reac-
tion of relief is expressed in booming laughter or silent
tears, the inner feeling is one of joy and gratitude." [5]

No individual, family, or nation has ever been the
worse because of the experience of rebirth. The con-
trary is true: When a person gets born again, he is
better off to himself, to his family, to his nation, and
to the world. Being born again will not make a person a great politician, athlete, or anything else. But
when a person has abilities in a given area and gets
born again, this change in his life will heighten what
abilities he has. When a person commits himself to
God, he finds that God challenges him to use his
abilities to the maximum (see Matt. 25:14-30).

The change of rebirth is sometimes spoken of as
conversion. Just a moment ago you read that Keith
Miller spoke of "the recently converted Christian."
Basically, a conversion is a change. We have dealt
with the person before the new birth, after the new
birth, and the fact that people can change. Now we

would do well to look at some key concepts in conversion to be sure that we understand the heart of the new birth experience that involves the changes we're talking about.

Key Concepts in Conversion

You can't stereotype conversion experiences. The changes involved in being born again catch up certain concepts that some of us tend to describe as steps to conversion: one, two, three, four. And the concepts perhaps involve a logical order. But being born again is like falling in love: the sequence of events may vary. For example, the very first time I ever saw my wife I had a feeling that she was the girl I might marry. She was on a date with a friend of mine, so the sequence of events that led us to meet, date, and eventually marry was not necessarily the same sequence that you or others may have gone through in getting married. But the basic concepts were probably pretty much the same.

More specifically, we might look at a 1976 nationwide Gallup survey that shows one person in three (34%) saying he has been born again. The people were asked, "Would you say that you have been born again or have had a born again experience—that is, a turning point in your life when you committed yourself to Christ?" Of those who responded, 48% were

Protestants, 18% Catholics; 28% men, 39% women; 27% had college, 36% high school, 42% grade school; 29% were 18-29 years old, 33% 30-49, 39% 50 and over; 23% from the East, 34% from the Midwest, 55% from the South, and 20% from the West. You don't have to know a lot to figure out that Protestants and Catholics differ quite a bit in their theology and what may be involved in being born again. But people from both groups heard the same question and agreed that they had been born again. The same thing is true of the other varied groups. So instead of looking primarily at exact steps, we will look at some key concepts of conversion by looking at some key terms.

Conviction: A person has to be convinced that there is something wrong in his life before he is likely to want to make any change. Psalm 51 is a vivid picture of a person who is convicted and convinced that he has done wrong. A study of the Bible reveals that God's Spirit is the one who brings conviction. When people compare themselves to other people, they tend to show up as pretty good citizens—at least, in their own minds. The only person worthy of comparison is Jesus Christ, and no person can measure up to this one and only sinless person. Against the pure life of Jesus, all other lives show up as soiled and dingy.

Luke 18:18-24 tells of a rich, young ruler who wanted that quality of life called *eternal.* A quick examination showed that the man was good by society's standards; however, he had the fault of loving money more than God. So many people know that they are not born again; their life is empty, hollow, boring, pointless, and they want to change. But all too often they don't see any wrong in their lives; and if the wrong becomes obvious, they may not be willing to commit themselves to Christ and let him change them. Conviction is necessary, but conviction alone is not salvation.

Repentance: Repentance is more than being sorry. There is the kind of repentance that is regret—such as being sorry you got a ticket for speeding. But the kind of repentance that leads to new life is a change of mind that results in a change of condition, attitudes, and actions. It is an about-face in life. The person who repents is one who makes a decision to turn from his sin and to turn to Jesus as a follower of his. Repentance is the key that unlocks the door to a person's whole life-style so that God can work the miracle of the new birth. Repentance is one facet of conversion: it is the turning point that directs a person toward God. Repentance is necessary for salvation (Matt. 3:2, 8; 4:17). But there is more to salvation than conviction and repentance.

Trust: The Bible says, "Believe on the Lord Jesus Christ, and thou shalt be saved" (Acts 16:31, KJV). This kind of belief is more than intellectual agreement that Jesus lived. The concept is *trust*. When a person entrusts his life and destiny to Jesus, then he believes with the kind of belief necessary for salvation and the kind of belief that produces change in his life.

Confession: Confession alone is not salvation. A person can confess that Jesus is Lord everyday and still not speak from the experience of being born again (Matt. 7:21-23). But tied with conviction, repentance, and trust, confession is a key concept in conversion. Romans 10:9-11 says, "If you confess with your lips that Jesus is Lord and believe in your heart that God raised him from the dead, you will be saved. For man believes with his heart and so is justified, and he confesses with his lips and so is saved. The scripture says, 'No one who believes in him will be put to shame!' " (RSV).

I used to hear a man confess his sins every week, but he showed no evidence of turning from them and doing anything about them. Confession without the other key concepts of conversion is powerless. But confession that Jesus is the object of your faith and the master of your life is important. And there is no real excuse for keeping that commitment secret. Someone has wisely said, "There is no such thing as secret discipleship; either the discipleship will destroy the secret, or the secret will destroy the discipleship."

Forgiveness: When a person responds to conviction

with repentance, trust, and confession, God forgives the person of all his sins and gives him a life that is new in time and in quality. The person is a new creation; he is born again.

People who are not born again don't know what they are missing. A friend of mine was driving in the Great Smoky Mountains one time. He and his wife were alone and had been driving for a long time when she pointed out that they were getting low on gas and that he ought to stop. He passed one gas station and then another, confident that he would know when it was time to get gas. As the gauge suddenly moved to empty and below empty, my friend knew that the next thing he would be hearing was, "I told you so." There wasn't another station in sight. But finally, when it seemed that the car would not go another mile, my friend came to the top of a hill and saw a gas station. You would have to be a husband in that predicament to know how relieved he was. When the old station attendant came out to fill up the gas tank, my friend said, "It's great to be alive, isn't it"—as he drew in a deep breath of mountain air. Without so much as lifting his head, the old attendant seriously answered, "I don't know; I ain't never been any other way."

But the born-again person knows the truth of the Scripture that says, "You he made alive, when you were dead through the trespasses and sins in which

you once walked, following the course of this world"
(Eph. 2:1-2, RSV). The person who gets born again
realizes what it was like to be dead because he knows
he was dead in his sins and trespasses; and he knows
what it is like to be spiritually alive.

Changes That Take Place

In the conversion experience, changes do take place.
A person receives salvation. He is saved from hell on
earth and in eternity. He is saved from a wasted and
harmful life on earth. He accepts Jesus as the master
of his life—that always goes with accepting Jesus as
Savior. He becomes the home of God's Spirit (Eph.
1:13-14; 4:30). These foundational changes take place
in everyone who becomes born again.

The born-again person is not perfect. He likely will
sin again, but he will not practice sin as a way of life
(1 John 3:6-9). He will not have all of his problems
solved; in fact, he may find he has more problems.
But he will have strength and guidance to deal with
those problems. He will find joy in knowing that his
life and destiny are secure with Jesus Christ. That's
a change worth making.

5. A New You

Be not conformed to this world: but be ye
transformed by the renewing of your mind,
that ye may prove what is that good, and
acceptable, and perfect, will of God (the
apostle Paul).

Christians are not born full grown. Their condition
and destiny are changed in a moment of commitment
to Jesus Christ, but the very fact of their new birth
calls for a continual changing and growing in their
thoughts and outlooks. The last chapter focused
primarily on how a person's condition changes when
he becomes a Christian. The chapter did not spell
out how being born again affects the inner person.
This chapter will focus on what happens after conversion: when a person gets a new mind-set and re-
fuses to be molded into the thought patterns of the
culture he lives in.

Paul wrote, "Let this mind be in you, which was
also in Christ Jesus" (Phil. 2:5, KJV). The New

Testament is full of thoughts that reveal Christ's kind of thinking. The Sermon on the Mount (Matt. 5–7) is one of the best places to go for an outline of the thoughts, attitudes, and actions that Jesus had and that he wants his followers to have. But there are many other places in the New Testament that tell about the inner person that every Christian ought to be. For example, Galatians 5:22-23 says, "The fruit of the Spirit is love, joy, peace, longsuffering, gentleness, goodness, faith, meekness, temperance" (KJV).

We won't be able to look at all the changes that ought to occur in a person who is born again, but we will look at some very basic changes in the thinking of those who really are Christians and who really do try to follow Christ. And before we get into those changes, we probably ought to look at a basic fact of the Christian life.

A Basic Fact

In the new birth experience we get a new nature, but we do not lose our human nature. When we receive spiritual life, we are new creations; and we are able to begin pleasing God (Rom. 8:6-9). But that does not mean we quit displeasing God. Paul himself wrote Romans 7:14-25 to tell everyone that he knew he wasn't perfect and that he needed help to match the commitment of his mind with everyday living (see especially Rom. 7:25). When a Christian falls short of his commitment to Jesus Christ, he does not get *un*born; rather, he needs to turn again from that disobedience or sin and ask forgiveness from God. As the old motto on my high school class ring reads, "Not failure but low aim is crime." The Christian is to turn his eyes upon Jesus; and every time he takes his eyes off the goal of Jesus, he is to come back with a renewed commitment.

Christians don't stay in the gutter of life. They may fall there, but they won't stay there if they really are Christians. I've watched hogs and I've watched sheep. The hogs are content to slop around in the mud and filth all day long. That is their nature. Sheep may fall into the mud, but they are anxious to get out of it; that is their nature. If we were hogs before we became Christians, then our new nature is that of sheep.

If we are sure that we are genuinely committed to Christ, then we ought not to doubt our salvation or our past experience of being born again.

Some people teach that you weren't really born again unless you can recall the day and time and place where that experience took place. I suppose most Christians are able to share that information. However, I heard of a man who had a faulty memory but a strong commitment to Christ; and he could not supply all of that information. His reply to the question

was: "I don't remember the first time I was born
either, but I know I was born."

There are evidences that indicate whether a person
has been born again. But the evidences are best used
for self-examination and not for judging the spiritual
condition of others. God, not man, is to be the judge.
We have the epistles of 1, 2, and 3 John to help us
know whether we've been born again. These epistles
speak of loving one another as well as of loving God,
of believing what is right, and of doing what is right.
So they can help a person determine his spiritual
condition. But let's move on to consider the new
you that comes into being when you follow the
divine design for living.

A New Mind

A new mind has new attitudes and thoughts that
arise out of a commitment to God through following
Christ. The commitment is a trust that Christ is divine and really does know what is best for us in each
instance. Spiritual salvation is permanent, but the
level of commitment to Christ varies. (We see this
in the church at Ephesus, which was described as
having left its first love; read Rev. 2:1-7.) We have
an old mind that does not leave us when we become a
Christian, but that old mind is to be constantly in the
process of renewal.

New Christians want to be perfect now, and that want-to is good. But new Christians don't have to try to live their faith for very long before they find out that although they have won the war, the battle for their mind continues on a day-by-day basis. Christians are not what they dream of being, but they can balance future dreams with present realities. Scott Fitzgerald wrote of the autobiographical Amory Blaine, "It was always the becoming he dreamed of, never the being." [1] The point is that some folks are so busy and anxious about becoming that they fail to enjoy being. Someone has said, "That is a pleasant pilgrimage in which the journey itself is part of the destination." There ought to be some joy both in being and in becoming. As you read some of the things that characterize mature Christians, you can share in the joy of what you are as a born-again person; and you can also dream of what you can become in the power of Christ.

When a person is born again, the experience he has had and the beliefs he holds can help him overcome fear, self-centeredness, hostility, greed, prejudice, insecurity, jealousy, resentment, lack of forgiveness, and a lot of other mind-crippling attitudes. (These inner attitudes show up in external symptoms, and we'll look at some of those symptoms in the next chapter. Perhaps a series of contrasts will give us insights to how a born-again person may become new.

Security vs. Insecurity

All around us we see contrasts between security and insecurity. Christ provides Christians with a security that nothing and no one can ever take away (Rom. 8:32-39). If you were to take the time to make a list of all the things you know people are insecure about, that list would be a long one. People are insecure about marriage, their jobs, their health, the economy, the political scene, self-image, decision-making, morality, spiritual condition, and the long list of specifics that you and other readers could add.

Insecurity gnaws at the mind and the stomach; it erodes the vitality of personality. Some people have lived with insecurity so long that they are uncomfortable without it. Last week a friend of mine said, "Things are going so well that it makes me wonder how long it's going to last." He was perhaps just being realistic, but he wasn't focusing on Jesus' teaching: "Do not be anxious about tomorrow, for tomorrow will be anxious for itself. Let the day's own trouble be sufficient for the day" (Matt. 6:34, RSV).

Trouble will come to every life, and it may come to stay for as long as you live. The security a Christian has comes in knowing that he will be able to meet trouble, deal with it, and live with it if necessary. Death? It means the end of physical existence and of life as we know it. But for the Christian, not even death is a cause for insecurity. Paul wrote: "The last enemy to be destroyed is death" (1 Cor. 15:26, RSV). He added: "This perishable nature must put on the imperishable, and this mortal nature must put on immortality. When the perishable puts on the imperishable, and the mortal puts on immortality, then shall come to pass the saying that is written:

'Death is swallowed up in victory.'

'O death, where is thy victory?

O death, where is thy sting?'

The sting of death is sin, and the power of sin is the law. But thanks be to God, who gives us the victory through our Lord Jesus Christ" (1 Cor. 15:53-57, RSV).

The victory that we have over death is life. In being born again we gain a quality of life (eternal life) that death cannot conquer. After the Christian's physical death, there is life on a higher plane than ever before. Even though eternal life begins the moment a person becomes a Christian, it is heightened for the Christian beyond this life. One of the best statements of this heightened life is in Revelation 21:4-5: "God shall wipe away all tears from their eyes; and there shall be no more death, neither sorrow, nor crying, neither shall there be any more pain: for the former things are passed away. And he that sat upon the throne said, Behold, I make all things new.

And he said unto me, Write: for these words are true
and faithful" (KJV).

God did not intend for us to live in insecurity. Although Jesus knew that he would die upon a cross, he
told his disciples, "Peace I leave with you, my peace I
give unto you: not as the world giveth, give I unto you.
Let not your heart be troubled, neither let it be afraid"
(John 14:27, KJV). Jesus had the kind of peace that
knew God was in charge no matter what man or Satan
might do. He had a peace that did not depend on changing circumstances. Jesus had security, and he obviously
wanted his followers to have that same kind of security.

Sometimes Christians forget. But when Christians
rest in the security God has provided for them, they
are a happy and peaceful people. They can put up with
the present, meet it, and overcome it because they know
that God has the last word; and that last word is a good
one for Christians.

Jesus was secure, but he was also concerned. He
cried inwardly when the people of Jerusalem chose
spiritual death instead of spiritual life (Matt. 23:37).
As a Christian you won't quit having concerns. Christians do sometimes divorce, lose their jobs, get termi-
nal illnesses, and suffer just as non-Christians do. Christians hurt. But they have someone to help them in
their hurt. They have the living Christ, and they have
Christian friends. And they have a mind-set that lets
them look beyond the present.

Faith vs. Fear

Fear is closely related to insecurity, but the object of fear may be obvious. When anything openly threatens life or safety, fear is a natural emotion. Fear as a way of life is not an emotion that a person ought to have. And faith in Christ can help a person overcome fear. I know that by personal experience.

I was leaving Nashville one evening about dusk. The jet plane I was on was more than halfway down the runway when it began to vibrate as if it would come apart. Since it was too early for luggage to settle and I had been on that relatively smooth runway many times before, I became apprehensive and my stomach tightened. But after a few seconds of violent shaking, the plane lifted smoothly into the air. I breathed a sigh of relief as I thought about my flight to Pittsburgh and then on to Detroit.

The flight attendants soon began to appear with food trays and smiles. Everything was OK. The food was good, and the flight was smooth. Then it came time to land. The pilot's voice came over the intercom: "I don't know whether you are aware of what happened when we left Nashville. We blew a front tire, and we may not have power in the landing gear; so we'll have to prepare for an emergency landing. Please follow the instructions of the flight attendants."

I was afraid. The possibility of disaster came home

as passengers obediently took false teeth out and eye-
glasses off and bent over in a braced position. I didn't
have false teeth, and I wasn't about to take my glasses
off—as nearsighted as I was. But one of the flight attendants came by and took my glasses off.

I sat in nearsighted blindness in a crash position,
and I had a few moments to think. My memory went
back to my wife, Phyllis, and my three boys I had left
in Nashville. I didn't want to leave a widow and three
sons without a dad. But I knew they were all right.
I was well insured, and each member of my family had
already become a Christian. So I felt secure for them.
Then I thought through my life from boyhood days
until the present. My fear slipped away as I remem-
bered how I had exercised faith and had been born
again as a young boy. I recalled the verse of Scripture
that I had read, memorized, and believed: "For God
so loved the world, that he gave his only begotten Son,
that whosoever believeth in him should not perish, but
have everlasting life" (John 3:16, KJV).

My childish faith wasn't anything spectacular. I
wasn't old enough to have done much of anything
that people considered to be sin. But I had heard
enough and read enough of the Bible to know that I
had rebelled against God. I had disobeyed God. I had
lied. And I wasn't at peace with God. So in a moment
of decision, I committed all of me that I knew how to
commit in trusting Jesus as my Master and Savior.

The best I remember, I told the pastor, "I want to be a Christian." And from that time on I had an assurance that nothing could take eternal life away from me, and nothing could take me away from God and his love.

Quickly then my mind raced on to think of my teenage years. The youth years had gone quickly, and two Scriptures stood out as turning points in my life. One of those Scriptures was, "I press toward the mark for the prize of the high calling of God in Christ Jesus" (Phil. 3:14, KJV). I was a typical youth, and no one would have mistaken me for a saint. While I had not lost my new birth experience, I had moved more than a step away from the joy of my salvation. As I watched the non-Christians around me, I realized I could have been mistaken for one of them. My Christianity scarcely showed at all, except for the fact that I went to church with my parents. Just as I had once dedicated my life, I rededicated my life and made Philippians 3:14 one of the mottoes of my life. As I got serious about trying to find and do the will of God, I found myself saying, "I can't do that!" Then I read Philippians 4:13: "I can do all things through Christ which strengtheneth me" (KJV). And I found myself doing things I never thought I could. I rediscovered the joy of my salvation and found new purpose in life.

In four short years of college, I got a wife, two sons, and a college degree from Baylor University. Then I went on to graduate school, and in another four years I got another degree and another son. But at the same time I worked myself to exhaustion. I couldn't see how a Christian could be anxious about all the things I was anxious about, and I shared that thought with my Christian doctor. He said, "Johnnie, you don't have a faith problem; you have a physical problem. You've just overdone it and need some rest." And I read, "Cast all your anxieties on him, for he cares about you" (1 Pet. 5:7, RSV). I did just that, and I got my physical and emotional strength back.

It is interesting to notice that in a few moments of memory, I recalled a Scripture to match every turning point or crisis in my life. And as I recalled those Scriptures and turning points, a peace came over me; and my fear was gone. I wasn't anxious to die, but I wasn't afraid to either.

The moment of truth came as the plane touched down. The flat-tire landing was rough, but the gear held; and everyone was OK. The passengers clapped for the pilot, and the group of strangers smiled at each other as if they had been longtime friends. And at least one passenger had learned through experience that his faith could conquer fear.

Fear is not a one-time thing. It comes again and again to most of us. But if we practice faith as a way of life, we can overcome fear every time.

I don't know what you might be afraid of; but if

you are afraid of anything, imagine how it would be
to relax from your fear and have faith that God con-
trols your destiny. That kind of faith does away with
unnecessary fear, and it helps us to face and overcome
and see beyond circumstances that we dread.

In 1975 thieves stole millions of dollars from a
London bank's safety-deposit boxes. One woman who
lost $480,000 worth of jewelry from her deposit box
said, "Everything I've got was in there. My whole life
was in that box." She had lost her security and feared
the future. The person who is born again has his life
wrapped up in commitment to Christ, not things; and
he simply can't lose his security. Nor does he have
reason to fear the future. Becoming a Christian changes
a person's sense of values and really does help the person to become new in how he views life. The new person gets a new set of personal convictions.

Convictions vs. Hang-ups

When a person gets born again, he is a living paradox.
He has accepted Christ as his Master, which implies
that he is Christ's slave. Yet, he is more free than he
has ever been in his life. He has security and a freeing
faith.

A hang-up is usually thought of as something that
causes a person mental or emotional difficulties. The
easiest advice to give is this: Get rid of your hang-ups.

But there are good hang-ups as well as bad hang-ups. When people have convictions and go against those convictions, they suffer mental or emotional distress. So, in a way, convictions could be considered hang-ups. Good hang-ups hold us up and lift us over much of the wrong in life. Bad hang-ups hold us back from living freely and joyously. So, in a nutshell, we need to get rid of our bad hang-ups and keep our good ones.

Bad hang-ups are inhibitions and guilt feelings brought about by our upbringing and our culture. They keep us from living life at its best. A lot of Christians and others need to be freed up from bad hang-ups. And nothing will free a person from bad hang-ups quicker and better than a study of God's Word.

False guilt is something created by man but unsupported by God. When a person gets born again, he ties his convictions to the God of the Bible, not to the changing viewpoints of mere human beings. Each generation has people who seem to think they have discovered new ways of behavior when they are actually advocating or repeating what other generations have practiced before. These people often denounce God, the church, traditional morality, and the Ten Commandments as if they themselves were gods. Their categorical condemnation of Bible truths may sound wise to some; but to those who are students of the Bible, history, and human nature, the self-appointed moral messiahs are just fooling themselves. In the Bible Christians find God's value system for mankind. And it is what is best for mankind.

You would expect to read what you have just read from one who has experienced the new birth, wouldn't you? But Dr. Donald T. Campbell, former president of the American Psychological Association, chided his fellow psychologists for siding with self-gratification over self-restraint and for regarding guilt as a neurotic symptom. He pointed out that psychiatrists and psychologists had assumed that human impulses provided by biological evolution are right and that repressive or inhibiting moral traditions are not. Then he went on to say that in his judgment the assumption you've just read is *scientifically* wrong ("Morals Make a Comeback," *Time,* Sept. 15, 1975: 94).

Good hang-ups are inhibitions that fit the guidance for good living which we find in God's Word. The person with no inhibitions lacks the moral standards of the Bible and denies the responsibility of being a person created in the image of God. The person with good hang-ups has a value system built on God's standards. His hang-ups lift him up and help him live constructively. By society's standards, good and bad change with the times. But by God's standards, good and bad stand in stark contrast. The Christian is one who has Bible-based convictions.

96 What It Means to Be Born Again

Self-denial vs. Self-indulgence

Jesus said, "If any man will come after me, let him
deny himself, and take up his cross daily, and follow
me. For whosoever will save his life shall lose it; but
whosoever will lose his life for my sake, the same shall
save it" (Luke 9:23-24, KJV). We don't have the space
to go into all the meaning of this paradox, but we can
get to the heart of part of the meaning.

When a person lives for himself instead of for others,
he tends to be miserable; and that selfishness diminishes
his own life. The person who sacrifices his own com-
fort and convenience to live for others tends to find
life at its best. The emotionally healthy people I know
are those who live beyond themselves. The emotional
cripples are those who indulge themselves, think of
themselves all of the time, and scarcely ever move outside their own little shell of a world.

The world is full of both kinds of people: the self-
denying and the self-indulgent; and it is fuller of the
latter. But those who show one of the characteristics
of being born again are the self-denying. Let me tell
you about one of them. His name is Copper. He was
pressed financially during one very trying time in his
life. And the most amazing thing happened: He won
a new Mustang in a drawing at a local grocery store.
What would you have done if you had been Copper?
Well, he sold the car. And when a young college

student who didn't have enough money to pay his tuition opened up his mail, he found a check for several hundred dollars and a note that read: "Praise God from whom all good Mustangs flow." I know all of Copper's debts didn't get paid right then, but my tuition did. And that was just one example of that Christian's magnificent obsession to deny himself and help others—without letting anyone else know about his good deeds.

When people get converted, they really do change. Their attitudes change, and they begin to focus on others instead of spending all their thoughts and money on themselves. And there are other signs that reflect something of a person's spiritual condition.

Truth vs. Falsehood

The Bible says, "Ye shall know the truth, and the truth shall make you free" (John 8:32, KJV). When a person becomes a new creation in his commitment to Christ, he also becomes a person of integrity. He may openly say that he will not ever knowingly tell a lie, for he recognizes the importance of living a life that is consistent with the life of Christ. And Christ said, "I am the way, the truth, and the life" (John 14:6, KJV). The person who tells the truth is freed from the nagging concern about covering up past lies.

Falsehood enslaves the liar. And once a person tells a lie that becomes known as a lie, he leaves others uncertain about whether he is ever telling the truth. Lying creates anxiety, wastes energy, and causes a deadness in relationships. Truth does just the opposite.

Ephesians 4:15 tells us that we are to speak the truth in love. Some people pride themselves on being frank, and they are brutally frank. They are honest but tactless. The kind of truth that expresses the mind of Christ is truth spoken in a spirit of love.

There are many other contrasting attitudes that reflect differences in those who are dedicated followers of Christ and those who are not: proud vs. humble, forgiving vs. unforgiving, merciful vs. unmerciful, and so forth. But there is a foundational attitude that characterizes the dedicated Christian and shows that he is a new person.

Love

Love can be the opposite of hate; but, as others have observed, it is more often the opposite of indifference. The behavior of love is portrayed fully and beautifully in 1 Corinthians 13. When a person loves with the kind of love described in 1 Corinthians 13, he shows that he is born again. The heart of that chapter says: "Love is patient; love is kind and envies no one. Love is never boastful, nor conceited, nor rude; never selfish, not quick to take offence. Love keeps no score of wrongs; does not gloat over other men's sins, but delights in the truth. There is nothing love cannot face; there is no limit to its faith, its hope, and its endurance" (1 Cor. 13:4-7, NEB).

In thinking about attitudes, you've read just a few of the characteristics of a renewed mind. When a person becomes a Christian, he is like a newborn baby: He is a new creation, but he is not full grown. He has to cultivate the attitudes that God wants him to have. After he matures, he may slip back into spiritually childish behavior. Nevertheless, he is a new creature who has the potential of renewing his mind so that it will be patterned after the mind of Christ. The change of mind is a logical consequence of being born again, but the change is not automatic and permanent as far as attitudes go. That's why Paul wrote Romans 12:2, which you read at the beginning of this chapter. Now, read that same verse in another translation as we conclude this chapter:

"Don't let the world around you squeeze you into its own mold, but let God remold your minds from within, so that you may prove in practice that the plan of God for you is good, meets all his demands and moves toward the goal of true maturity" (Phillips).

6. A Fresh Look at Life

Just as a writer has the right to expect that his novel will not be judged by one page, so does a person have the right to expect that his life will not be judged by one page—one day, one deed, or one season—but by its totality.

Can people really change? Can they really have an experience that will give them a fresh perspective on life? Can they really become new persons? The answer is yes! And I've tried to illustrate that truth in earlier chapters. People can become new in beliefs, attitudes, behavior, and interpersonal relationships. So far we have focused mostly on the changes that occur in the inner person. This chapter will not leave those emphases, but it will build on them to show the fresh look at life that characterizes Christians. The chapter will explain what being born again means to interpersonal relationships and to the working out of the new birth experience.

When a person gets born again, he becomes a new person; but he is still a human being. Sometimes he may not think, act, or talk like a Christian. But if we look at the whole of a Christian's life and quit criticizing one or more pages, we should be able to tell that he is a Christian. How? We can see how he spends his time, his money, and his energy. We can look at his life against the mirror of the Bible. And we can look in this chapter at some specific evidences that usually indicate if a person is a Christian.

New Relationships

Getting along with people is a skill that everyone needs to develop, but it is a skill that should come easier to Christians than to non-Christians. I do not mean that Christians won't have conflicts; they will have conflicts sometimes just because they are Christians—as Christ did. But when a person has the spirit of Christ in him, he has a new vision of what relationships can be. He not only sees people for what they are; he sees them for what they can become.

Jimmy Carter said, "We have a tendency to exalt ourselves and to dwell on the weaknesses and mistakes of others. I have come to realize that in every person there is something fine and pure and noble, along with a desire for self-fulfillment. Political and religious leaders must attempt to provide a society within which these human attributes can be nurtured and enhanced." [1]

The apostle Paul said something like that in the Bible: "By the grace given to me I bid every one among you not to think of himself more highly than he ought to think, but to think with sober judgment, each according to the measure of faith which God has assigned him. For as in one body we have many members, and all the members do not have the same function, so we, though many, are one body in Christ, and individually members one of another. Having gifts that differ according to the grace given to us, let us use them . . . . Let love be genuine; hate what is evil, hold fast to what is good; love one another with brotherly affection; outdo one another in showing honor" (Rom. 12:3-6, 9-10, RSV).

When a person is born spiritually, his relationship to God changes; and his relationship to other people changes. The new relationships may not be as obvious to the new Christian as they are to others. I heard of a woman who was irritable and had trouble getting along with other people. Finally, a doctor prescribed some tranquilizers for her and told her to come back and see him in a few days. When the woman returned for her next visit, the doctor asked her if she could tell any difference in herself after taking the prescription. She said, "No, I can't tell any difference in myself; but other folks sure have started acting a lot nicer."

And sometimes that's the way it is in the life of one who has a new relationship to God and a new relationship to his fellowman.

What about those who claim to be Christians and still have trouble getting along with others? We are still human, aren't we? The apostle Paul, who wasn't always easy to get along with, wrote: "Lead a life worthy of the calling to which you have been called, . . . forbearing one another in love, eager to maintain the unity of the Spirit in the bond of peace" (Eph. 4:1-3, RSV). "Forbearing one another in love" can be translated "putting up with one another in love." Personalities and circumstances can still be sources of conflict for Christians. But Christians are to keep on loving one another even when they differ.

Most relationship problems for Christians seem to grow out of miscommunication or misunderstanding of circumstances. A popular saying that reflects the problem people have in communicating goes like this: *I know you believe you understand what you think I said, but I am not sure you realize that what you heard is not what I meant.* Mature Christians give others the benefit of a doubt when words don't communicate. And as far as circumstances go, mature Christians learn to have an attitude of being sensitive to others' unknown hurts. We never know what people have gone through unless we have been able to walk beside them all the way.

When you meet someone wearing a frown,
He may be climbing a hill
  while you're coming down.
When you meet someone wearing a frown,
He may be in a storm
  while you're in one of life's calms.

How little do we know what makes people the way
they are! But we can love them. And that love is to
characterize a Christian as he relates to Christians and
non-Christians alike.

New Behavior

Matching Christian beliefs with Christian behavior is
a big job. Being born again is not a theory that needs
proving; it is an experience that needs to be lived out
in daily life. Theology (religious beliefs) must serve
as the foundation for ethics and morals (behavior).
Although the Bible doesn't spell out every detail of
how a person is supposed to live, it does give principles
that will guide the Christian in all of life.

But there are problems in matching beliefs with behavior—more than just the problem of being human.
People may believe the same biblical truths but interpret their application in different ways. The important
thing is that the new birth causes a person to look at
himself in the mirror of God's will as it is revealed in

the Bible. And the Christian is to keep on looking in
that mirror as long as he lives.

One person wrote, "If mirrors served only to show
us images of things *exactly as they are,* they would be
used sparingly. Who needs a mere reflection when the
world can be observed directly? But looking-glasses
reveal more than simple reality. They stimulate our
imaginations. They give us fresh perspectives. They
disclose not only the actual, but the possible, too.
They make us look at things and at ourselves more
closely; more critically. And by changing our viewpoints, they help to change our interests, our minds,
and even our lives." [2]

A mirror lets us see what we are, but it also lets
us see what we can become. The Bible says, "Don't,
I beg you, only hear the message, but put it into practice; otherwise you are merely deluding yourselves.
The man who simply hears and does nothing about it
is like a man catching the reflection of his own face
in a mirror. He sees himself, it is true, but he goes on
with whatever he was doing without the slightest recol-
lection of what sort of person he saw in the mirror.
But the man who looks into the perfect mirror of God's
law, the law of liberty, and makes a habit of so doing,
is not the man who sees and forgets. He puts that law
into practice and he wins true happiness" (Jas. 1:22-25,
Phillips).

The apostle Paul wrote, "At present we are men

looking at puzzling reflections in a mirror. The time will come when we shall see reality whole and face to face! At present all I know is a little fraction of the truth, but the time will come when I shall know it as fully as God now knows me!" (1 Cor. 13:12, Phillips).

These Bible passages combine to say that a Christian's beliefs are to show up in the way he lives. The passages call for taking a fresh look at life on a regular basis. It's easy for Christians to get stale and then fail to grow as they should.

In *Why Not the Best?* Jimmy Carter admitted, "A few years ago I was sitting in church in Plains thinking about the title of the morning sermon. I do not remember anything our pastor had to say that morning, but I have never forgotten the title of the sermon: 'If you were arrested for being a Christian, would there be enough evidence to convict you?'

"I was then a member of the largest and most prestigious church in town, a Sunday School teacher and a deacon, and I professed to be quite concerned about my religious duties. But when asked that question I finally decided that if arrested and charged with being a committed follower of God, I could probably talk my way out of it! It was a sobering thought." [3] Jimmy Carter looked in the mirror and was led to make some changes in his life. And that's at the heart of the growth process for every newborn Christian.

Finding a Church Home

I've purposely avoided saying too much about becoming a member of a local church because it is easy
to confuse getting your name on a church roll with
the experience of being born again. If a person gets
his name on a church roll and does not have the experience of being born again, he is a counterfeit Christian. But if a person gets born again and does not
identify with a local church, then he is being dis-
obedient to his commitment to Christ.

There are people who say you can be just as good
a Christian at home or on the lake as you can in
church. I wouldn't argue with that, but I would
point to the importance of the church and form my
own interpretation in light of that importance. Paul
said, "Take heed to yourself and to all the flock, in
which the Holy Spirit has made you guardians, to feed
the church of the Lord which he obtained with his own
blood" (Acts 20:28, RSV). Then the writer of Hebrews
wrote: "Let us hold fast the confession of our hope
without wavering, for he who promised is faithful;
and let us consider how to stir up one another to love
and good works, not neglecting to meet together, as
is the habit of some, but encouraging one another,
and all the more as you see the Day drawing near"
(Heb. 10:23-25, RSV).

Christ considered the church important enough to

die for it. He is the head of the church. Individual
churches may be weak and indifferent or strong and
dynamic; but we can't afford to condemn the church
that God has called us to be a part of.

Further, the church provides us a fellowship that
helps us to be faithful in our beliefs, to have a loving
spirit, and to band together to do good works. Isolated
Christians can easily get off into left field in both beliefs and behavior. If they place their lives in the
context of a Christian community, they have a sound-
ing board for beliefs and behavior. They are still individually responsible for what they believe and do, but
they are able to find out how others interpret the
Bible and apply those truths to daily living. So it
seems very important for a Christian to find a church
home and to identify himself with that church's mis-
sion.

Looking at Life as a Trust

Life is a trust from God. A few years ago, I did
something I had always wanted to do but had never
been able to finish: I read the Bible all the way through.
The reading took place over a year. As I reflected on
what I had read, I became intensely aware of the need
to depend on God and to realize that my life, my pos-
sessions, and all I had were a trust from God.

In the Bible, I read about people who lived for years

on end as if God did not exist. They lived life just as
they wanted to live it. They sinned, and lightning did
not strike them dead in the next instant. But there was
a cycle of rebellion against God, ruin, repentance, and
rebirth. The people in the Bible eventually paid for
their rebellion, and there always came a time when
they needed God. That profound thought has stayed
with me as I read about people doing away with God's
standards and then saying, "See, lightning didn't strike
me: it's OK." Life is a trust from God, and he holds
us responsible for that trust. (Again, read Matt. 25:
14-30.)

With a plea of concern, God said, "Can a maid forget her ornaments, or a bride her attire? yet my people have forgotten me days without number" (Jer.
2:32, KJV). Although salvation is a gift from God,
receiving that gift involves a voluntary commitment
to Christ and his way of living. Christ lived life as a
trust from God, and that's the way we're to live.

When a person is born again, that fact shows up in
the way he spends his time, his money, his energy,
and all of life. It shows up in the person's value system.
Look at the life of a man called Zacchaeus. He gladly
received Jesus and then said, "Lord, the half of my
goods I give to the poor, and if I have taken any thing
from any man by false accusation, I restore him four-
fold" (Luke 19:8, KJV). Seemingly, Zacchaeus had
lived to make money; but his value system changed,

and he saw how to use money as a follower of Jesus should use it. Friends may change. The whole balance of life may change. The Christian who is mature recognizes that there is a time for everything, and he puts Christ first.

A New Vocabulary

The Christian gets a new vocabulary. As he studies the Bible and goes to church, he will learn the meaning of words that were relatively meaningless to him before. He doesn't have to learn a stained-glass language or one that won't communicate in everyday life. In fact, the language of the New Testament was the ordinary, people-talk language of that day. Perhaps what I am talking about here is more of a new emphasis than a new vocabulary. Some of the words the new Christian begins to use in a fresh way are: Lord, Savior, self-denial, repentance, commitment, stewardship, eternal life, faith, hope, love. And there are a lot of other words that we could add to the list. At the same time, there are a lot of words that new Christians tend to delete from their vocabulary: words that aren't fit for Christians to use, no matter what other people say.

Clarence L. Barnhart has said, "Vocabulary is an index to a civilization, and ours is a disturbed one." Granville Hicks wrote, "Language reflects men's minds, and there are a lot of messy minds in the world." In

Webster's Collegiate Thesaurus (first published in Apr., 1976), the word *intoxicated* has more synonyms than any other word listed. One of the editors at Merriam-Webster's told me that this fact is a reflection on our society. Our everyday speech that we read and hear is polluted with words that people did not use in polite society a few years ago. I would be the last to judge all that a person should say or shouldn't say and what words he should use. But I do know that when a person gets born again, the experience affects how he speaks to others and what words he chooses to use. Paul wrote, "In these you once walked, when you lived in them. But now put them all away: anger, wrath, malice, slander, and foul talk from your mouth" (Col. 3:7-8, RSV).

A Fresh Look at Home

Christian homes are not perfect, and Christians sometimes get divorces. But the most successful homes I know anything about are Christian homes. Openly, we see that there is one divorce for roughly every three marriages; and privately there must be a lot of emotional divorce in the home that never shows up in a divorce court. Becoming a Christian is not a cure-all for every troubled home, but becoming a Christian does affect the home and the perspectives of those in the home.

According to the Bible, God's ideal is for those who marry to live life together and not leave each other. While they are not to exclude others from friendship, they are to commit themselves to each other with a love that excludes sexual relations with anyone else. This is God's ideal that does not change with man's improvisions.

Ideally, a marriage and the love in that marriage just keep on growing. But a lot of things can go wrong with the ideal. In marriage ceremonies, a bride and groom pledge themselves to each other until death parts them. But the marriage may die before the people do. Attitudes and feelings in a marriage may get sick. The irritations of time can wear down the sensitive people who joined their lives together in marriage. But when a marriage begins to lose its vitality and gets sick, commitment to God can keep the marriage together until it can get well or be reborn. Christians who stay close to Christ tend to stay close to their mates.

When children grow up in a home where there is commitment to God on the part of both parents and an obvious commitment and love between the parents, the children usually have the healthiest environment possible.

The same God who promises life beyond death can perform miracles in relationships within the home. His presence adds a new dimension to marriage.

There's so much more to say about becoming a Christian and its effect upon the home, but perhaps these few words may cause you or someone else to know that marriage can last; and it can be the kind of marriage that keeps on growing instead of merely enduring.

Dealing with Circumstances

The Christian life is the greatest life in the world. I believe that, and so do millions of other people. However, the Christian life is not an easy life; it is filled with temptations, problems, and unexplainable circumstances. The Christian doesn't have all the answers to what happens in life.

We could look at a lot of examples to illustrate what I'm talking about, but I'll try to condense the point: Becoming a Christian won't do away with all of your problems.

Cancer in the lives of people of all ages is one of the hardest things to understand. If a person smokes, drinks alcoholic beverages, and abuses his body, it stands to reason that he may get cancer or some other disease. But I've personally known a number of dedicated Christians who have died with cancer; and many of those people have been young people, people who took care of their bodies and lived the best life they could. For five years I watched a young

mother of three children die before she was thirty
years old. Why? I don't know. A young minister
friend of mine died of cancer in the prime of his
career. Why? I don't know.

There are accidents, murders, divorces, alcoholism,
and many other things that occur for which I don't
have a pat answer. But when life and death have done
their worst, the Christian is the one who endures and
will not be conquered. The Christian has this promise:
"We know that in everything God works for good with
those who love him, who are called according to his
purpose . . . . to be conformed to the image of his
Son" (Rom. 8:28-29, RSV).

The Alcoholics Anonymous prayer says, "O God,
give us serenity to accept what cannot be changed,
courage to change what should be changed, and wisdom to distinguish the one from the other." (Some
sources credit Reinhold Niebuhr with the prayer.)
The Christian is not a fatalist; he believes that circumstances can be changed. But when circumstances
are not changed, he doesn't quit believing in God.
He recognizes that the mind of man is no match for
the mind of God; one is finite and limited, the other
infinite and limitless.

What can a person do in the face of life's circumstances? He can do all he can, and he can pray. Many
people feel that whatever happens in life is the will of
God. Such a view reduces prayer to a time of express-

ing resignation that things cannot be changed. If whatever will be will be, there is no use in praying prayers of request. But all the Bible teaches that prayer can cause changes. Should we try to force our will on God through prayer? No. But we are to persistently and openly tell God what we think we need. In the will of God, prayer is a link that brings about changes. God has some blessings for us that we will not receive unless we pray for them.

Every prayer of asking is a prayer for a miracle. If we believe in any part of asking, we believe God can and does act within his creation and perform miracles. So our prayers of asking really involve degrees of faith for what we consider to be small or large miracles. But God can perform one miracle as easily as he can perform another. The problem for me is that I can't exercise faith as easily in prayer for an "incurable" disease as I can for a curable disease. So I am in the position of the one who prayed, "I believe; help my unbelief!" (Mark 9:24, RSV).

I believe in prayer; and, consequently, I believe in miracles. When God answers prayers the way I want him to, I thank him; when he does not, I recognize that I am human and God is God. To me, prayer is a mystery; but it is a wonderful mystery. And for those who are born again, it is a way of life in meeting and overcoming the circumstances of life that would crush us if we did not trust God.

Everyone who really lives has to face up to the complexity of life. In a moving and disturbing poem entitled "Simplicity," Jane Ann Webb concluded:

> *And don't try to tell me that when*
>   *I finally meet up with God, and say,*
>   *"God, finally! Tell me how,*
>   *and why, and what it's all about"—*
> *Don't try to tell me his reply will be,*
>   *"Well, you see,*
>   *It's really very simple . . . ."* 4

Life is not simple. But God makes sense out of life. And when life does not make sense, the Christian trusts that God does not make a mistake and that he knows the answers to the whys of life. The Christian has someone to trust! And that someone is trustworthy. Those who are born again know that they are born winners. God will take them in the defeat of life or the trauma of death and help them to see beyond the temporary. For the Christian, the final scene that endures forever is the scene of victory—victory over the circumstances of life and over the grave of death. Victory is at the heart of what it means to be born again. And the Christian's victory is tied up with the victory of Jesus Christ as he died on the cross, defeated sin, and was raised on the third day to live forever.

Serendipities in the Christian Life

Following Christ leads to serendipities. Are you
sensitive to serendipities? No, I am not talking about
your allergies. You can find a definition of serendipity
in a good dictionary. But the best way to understand
serendipity is to look at examples. So let's look at
some.

Columbus set out across the Atlantic to find Asia,
but he failed. However, in his pursuit of Asia, Columbus found something else: He stumbled on America.
You see, America was a serendipity for Columbus.

Louis Pasteur was searching for a way to keep wine
from turning sour when he discovered the life-saving
serendipity of pasteurization. Wilhelm Roentgen was
trying to improve photography and was led down the
serendipity trail to discover X-ray.

Edward Jenner once had a sweetheart who told him
she could not get smallpox because she had had cow-
pox when she was a child. Years later, Jenner recalled
that bit of country wisdom during a threatened smallpox epidemic. And he developed a safe vaccine for
smallpox.

An experimenter named Minot began to run out of
money to feed some dogs he was working with. So he
fed the dogs liver—the cheapest food available at that
time. In his studies, Minot discovered the liver was
doing something to the dogs' blood. Today we take

liver shots for anemia because of Minot's sensitivity to serendipity.

Saccharin? A chemist forgot to wash his hands before he ate a roast beef sandwich, and the sandwich tasted sweet. He went back to his laboratory and discovered the sweetest serendipity on record: saccharin.

You've just read about a few of the countless examples of serendipity. And you can read about many more serendipities in J. Wallace Hamilton's book *Serendipity* (Old Tappan, New Jersey: Fleming H. Revell Co., 1965). But I think you've probably got the idea: A serendipity is finding something wonderful while searching for something else. You see, serendipities are the unsought *happies* of life. They usually come to people who are searching for something and are sensitive to many things.

The strange thing about the Christian is that he is willing to give up everything to follow Christ; and as he follows Christ, he always gets more than he gives. The by-products of the Christian life are serendipities that enrich life. Although Jesus didn't use the term, he seemed to catch up the spirit of serendipity when he said: "Seek ye first the kingdom of God, and his righteousness; and all these things shall be added unto you" (Matt. 6:33, KJV).

The new birth really does provide a fresh look at life. You have to experience the new birth to get the whole new view. And when you do experience

the new birth, you will agree that it is good news.
That leads to what I have been saving for now.

Good News to Share

The Christian has received good news in being born
again, and it is the Christian's joy and job to share that
good news with everyone (Matt. 28:18-20; Rom. 1:
16-17). All people need to know Christ personally as
their Lord and Savior. They need the good news. And
good news is something to be told, not kept secret.

In the language of the Christian community, the
Christian is to be a witness. He has had an experience,
and he is to share that experience with others—not
argue about it. Many of those early Christians who
shared Christ have become known as martyrs. We
think of a martyr as someone who is persecuted for
his faith, and that thought is accurate. But the word
martyr came right over into English from the Greek
word *martus*. And *martus* is the Greek word for
witness. Christians shared the good news as witnesses.
The good news called for turning away from selfish
living and rebellion against God to unselfish living
and commitment to God. Those who would not
receive the good news were condemned and haunted
by its message. And they persecuted the witnesses.
So it was not long before witnesses and martyrs were
practically synonymous.

Today, Christians are persecuted for witnessing in some parts of the world. But most of us don't suffer anything more damaging than raised eyebrows and hurt egos when people react negatively to the good news. Yet, we are responsible for sharing our experience of being born again. And one of life's greatest joys is to share the news, see it received, and watch another person be born again.

The Great Christian Novel

Your life may not read like the great Christian novel. Your relationships and behavior may not always be what they ought to be. Your stewardship of life may have gaps and lapses. Your language may sometimes reflect your pre-Christian vocabulary. You may blunder at home and in dealing with circumstances. And you may have trouble identifying the serendipities that are supposed to be in your life and the witness that is to characterize you.

If you have accepted Christ as your Master and Savior, that one page of experience is more important than all of the other pages put together. Chances are that the other pages after that experience will read well too. Be that as it may, God is the author and finisher of your faith; and he will write the last chapter. And that last chapter will be a chapter of victory. Being born again provides a fresh look at life.

7. A Question for You

When the sands of time have run out in your life, you can't take the top off the hourglass and pour more sand in.

The final question is this: Have you been born again? This book is intended to be primarily explanatory from the author's perspective of what it means to be born again. However, the book can't help being personal, and this chapter is especially personal. I have shared my understanding and my experience of what it means to be born again. But I can't help wondering if you, the reader, have received and responded to the good news that God sent his Son to provide new life for everyone. That good news is more than a fact; it is an offer expecting a response.

People aren't argued into becoming Christians; they are loved into becoming Christians by the kind of concern God showed in giving his Son and by the kind of concern that tries to explain and then leave

the decision with the once-born person. Perhaps
some people are frightened into becoming Christians.
This chapter presents a question, not an argument; it
offers loving concern, not a threat to bring fear. It
offers some factors for you to consider if you have
never been born again or if you're not sure you've
had that experience. And if you are a Christian,
perhaps these factors will help you as you express
your concern to others who are not twice born.

Time Is a Factor

On a TV commercial the sand ran out of an hourglass; then someone removed the top and added some
more sand. I was amused. I also thought that it would
be nice if we could add some time when the time of
life has run out; but we can't. There comes a time to
die, and we die. Decision-making comes to an end.
The person who has not been born again has missed
his chance forever. So time is a factor that presents
an unknown limitation in deciding to accept Christ
and experience the new birth.

The Greek words *chronos* and *kairos* both mean
time, and they shed light on the *now* moments of life.
Chronos just means time—any old time. Our English
words *chronology, chronometer,* and *chronic* are
rooted in this general term. But *kairos* means season,
and it refers to the opportune time, the decisive mo-

ment, the now moment. *Kairos* is the Greek word used in "redeeming the time" in Ephesians 5:16 and Colossians 4:5 (KJV). The thought in those Bible passages is to make the most of time by seizing life's opportunities.

The *now* moments of life are like ripe fruit waiting to be picked. The choices we make in the critical moments of life determine life's super moments. The supreme super moment of life is the one in which a person chooses to accept Christ as his Lord and Savior. How you decide at the crosspoint of opportunity and decision is a matter of eternal life or eternal death. Some opportunities are like luggage on a conveyor belt at an airline: If you miss the first time around, the luggage keeps coming around. But not all opportunities are like that; and the opportunity to accept Christ is limited to the span of life. If you have not been born again, now is the opportune time.

The earlier in life a person takes advantage of the opportunity to become a Christian, the better off he is. He can start fulfilling God's design for his life and live life at its best. (How early in life a person can become a Christian is something I don't know, but I believe that is more a stage of development than a set age. When a person has rebelled against God and has been made aware of that and of the good news, he is in a position to make a decision to be born again.) As a rule, it is much easier for a youth to become a

Christian than it is for an adult; but usually the adult is the one who has less time and has the most critical need of being born again.

In *The Seasons of Life,* Paul Tournier said, "The further the season advances, the greater becomes the need to choose. To live is to choose. Those who through a childish notion of what fullness supplies want to lose nothing of their human inheritance, sacrifice nothing, give up nothing, lose out in spreading themselves too thin. They never attain true fullness." And he added, "The further on we go, the more we see time as a diminishing capital. Moreover, its running out goes on at an ever-quickening pace." [1]

Upon Richard Nixon's resignation from the presidency, a newscaster added, "And life goes on." A colleague of mine, barely in his thirties, died at the beginning of a workday when he suffered a massive heart attack. As the pall of death hung about us and we tried to do our work that day, another colleague commented, "And life goes on." But life doesn't always go on. There is an end to physical life. The born again go on to a fuller life, but those who are born only once go on to a deeper death from which there is no dying—spiritual death.

To me, two people who seemed ageless and unaffected by time were Jack Benny and Pablo Casals. Jack Benny always claimed to be 39; and when he

died, the news release stated, "Jack Benny finally
turned 40." As a rough average, 70 is a lifespan. When
the great musician Pablo Casals turned 70 and then 80
and then 90, people repeatedly asked him when he
would retire. Casals' unchanging answer was, "To retire means to die." When he died, the news release
about his death said, "At the age of 96, Don Pablo
Casals, the greatest musician of the century, retired."
Time is a factor in the life of everyone.

I have read that each story of a life ends with a
death. However, there is one story of a life that ended
with a new life—not a death! It is the story of Jesus
Christ. He was born, he lived, he died, and he was
raised from death on the third day (Matt. 28:5-6).
And all of us who experience being born again have
the promise that the story of our life will not end with
death, but with life (1 Cor. 15:19-22).

Theologian Karl Barth wrote: "The Easter message
tells us that our enemies, sin, the curse and death, are
beaten. Ultimately they can no longer start mischief.
They still behave as though the game were not decided,
the battle not fought; we must still reckon with them,
but fundamentally we must cease to fear them any
more." [2]

Time is a factor in decision-making, but for the
born again it is not a factor in the quality or quan-
tity of life. God has taken care of that through Christ
for those who commit themselves to Christ.

Understanding Is a Factor

A person may want to be born again but not understand how to be born again. Chapters 2 and 4 of this
book particularly focus on how to be born again. However, there are so many misconceptions about the new
birth that we need to clarify what makes a Christian.
William B. Small, a Methodist layman of Iowa, died,
leaving a will which provided that the income from
$75,000 of his estate should be used to benefit Chris-
tians. Ten of his relatives sued to break the will on
the ground that there is no way to determine what a
Christian is. And they won! Although many pastors,
priests, and professors testified, Judge Shannon B.
Charlton ruled that in his opinion a Christian cannot
be defined. This incident is just one evidence of the
hazy thinking that exists about what it means to be
a Christian.

In the first century, a Christian's beliefs and life
were so distinct that the name Christian was coined
to identify him (Acts 11:26). Today many people
wear the name Christian without living the life that
identifies Christians. Alexander the Great faced a
soldier who shared the name Alexander with him.
The soldier's behavior had been unacceptable. Alexander the Great is reported to have said, "Either change
your name or change your conduct." The same could
be said of those who claim to be Christians. There

seems to be little doubt that we can define how a person becomes a Christian and the behavior that characterizes a Christian.

What makes a Christian? Here are some reasonable but wrong answers: sincerity, goodness, comparison with the lives of others, and good works. People can be sincere and wrong. No one lives a perfect life, so no one is good enough to be saved on his own merit (see Rom. 3:10, 23). Jesus lived the only life that is worthy of comparison as far as salvation goes; he lived a perfect life. And no one can measure up to that comparison. Salvation is a gift that God has provided for us, and we can't work for it; rather, we work because of what we become in the new birth (Eph. 2:8-10).

Turning from self-will to God's will through accepting Jesus' death on the cross for us sounds too easy. Everyone knows you don't get anything free. Our salvation cost God the death of Christ on the cross, but *it is free to us*; and this gift is spoken of as God's grace. You have to accept salvation as a gift, or you can't have it at all. At the same time we accept Jesus as our Savior, we also accept him as Lord of our lives (Rom. 10:9-10). Salvation and lordship go together; you can't have one at the moment of salvation without the other. But part of God's mercy is that he doesn't cancel out our salvation when we disobey him. This understanding is basic information a person needs to answer the question of whether he has been born again. Now, let's look even further to see how a person can know whether he's been born again.

Reborn? How You Can Know

You may remember well the moment of your conversion or second birth; or you may not remember it very well. There are people who would take issue over what you've just read. However, the Bible teaches that right living, loving others, and believing God's truths are evidences that a person is born again. Read all of 1, 2, 3 John for the development of these thoughts. As a tree is known by the fruit it bears, so is a Christian known by the fruit he bears (Matt. 12:33; Gal. 5:22-23). A continuing relationship with Jesus Christ is evidence that a person is a Christian (John 15).

If ever there was a time when you truly committed your life to Christ and turned from your sin to his will, the Bible would say that you have become a Christian. If that's never happened, you need to be born again. Doubt about your experience is unnecessary. If you're not certain that you have become a Christian, you can make your commitment now.

Just as no two snowflakes are the same, no two conversion experiences may be expressed in the same way. But you can experience something similar to what Charles Colson experienced. He said, " 'Lord Jesus, I believe you. I accept you. Please come into my life. I commit it to you . . . .' With these words that morning, while the briny sea churned, came a sureness of mind that matched the depth of feeling in my heart. There came something more: strength and serenity, a wonderful new assurance about life, a fresh perception of myself and the world around me. In the process, I felt old fears, tensions, and animosities draining away. I was coming alive to things I'd never seen before, as if God was filling the barren void I'd known for so many months, filling it to its brim with a whole new kind of awareness." [3]

Have you been born again? You can know the answer to that question. You can know and respond about your commitment to Christ.

The Risk of Commitment

There is a risk to commitment. You can openly confess the decision of your heart and let others know that you have been born again. Then you will become painfully aware of your failure to live up to all that you're committed to. I've heard people say that they couldn't live up to the Christian life, but if they did decide to become Christians they would really "live it." Those people take Christianity seriously, and their intentions may be good. But they fail to understand that they will never be able to live a perfect life on earth, and they will never become Christians if they wait until they become good enough. Christians are people who take the risk of commitment and are better off now and forever because of it.

People may criticize you. But, as Theodore Roosevelt pointed out, it's not the critic who counts. The credit belongs to the man who is actually in the arena, who, at the worst, if he fails, at least fails while daring greatly, so that his place shall never be with those cold and timid souls who know neither victory nor defeat.

Students of football history will never forget Roy Riegels. In the 1929 Rose Bowl game between California and Georgia Tech, Tech fumbled on its own twenty-yard line. Riegels recovered the ball for Cal; and in the confusion he ran the wrong way with the ball until he was finally tackled by a teammate, Benny Lom, on his own one-yard line. Although people have alternately laughed and moaned over that incident, you have to give Roy Riegels credit for taking the risk of commitment and giving it his all—even though he ran in the wrong direction. And that's the kind of risk that Christ wants his followers to take. If we are willing to risk becoming fools for Christ, chances are that he can use us and keep us moving toward the right goal for his cause. Fear of failure is not reason enough for avoiding the new birth. You and I can say with the apostle Paul, "I can do all things in him who strengthens me" (Phil. 4:13, RSV).

Being born again is tied to the question of the meaning of existence. The question forces us to consider all of life and to separate tragedy from triviality—to get a proper focus on life.

Perspective: Tragedy vs. Triviality

Wouldn't it be enlightening if we could look at all the events of life at one time? We might find that what seemed to be a tragedy in life was really a triviality—or, at least, not nearly as bad as it seemed at the time when it happened. On the other hand, we might find that what seemed to be a triviality was a tragedy.

Tragedy or triviality? You may be under a mountain of work that causes you to feel that life is all work and no play. Your family may be having problems—financially or otherwise. Or you may have some personal problems that have just about gotten you down If you let life get gloomy whenever you have a problem, all of life may begin to look like a tragedy. Part of the answer to the problem is to get the right perspective. Look at your problem from the standpoint of a lifetime. Look at your problems as challenges. With that perspective, many of life's "tragedies" may take on the appearance of triviality.

God in his wisdom has kept us from seeing all of life

at once. But God's Word often emphasizes the
thought of looking at life as a whole. And this is
especially true in the matter of salvation. The greatest tragedy of all would be to live all of life and fail
to be born again. Against that possibility most of the
other bad things in life would appear to be trivial.
Those who are Christians have Christ to strengthen
them and guide them through other real tragedies of
life. Their day-by-day faith strengthens them for
the crises of life that eventually come to everyone.

The question about your spiritual condition is not
a trivial question. The answer is really between you
and God. But the Bible reveals that to reject Jesus
is life's supreme tragedy.

We read, "He came unto his own, and his own received him not" (John 1:11, KJV). And Jesus said,
"O Jerusalem, Jerusalem, killing the prophets and
stoning those who are sent to you! How often
would I have gathered your children together as a
hen gathers her brood under her wings, and you
would not! Behold, your house is forsaken and
desolate. For I tell you, you will not see me again,
until you say, 'Blessed be he who comes in the name
of the Lord' " (Matt. 23:37-39, RSV).

Joy, not tragedy, is the keynote of the Christian
life. Over and over again the Bible talks about the
joy that is designed for Christians. One example
of this design is stated in John 16:24: "Hitherto

have ye asked nothing in my name: ask, and ye shall receive, that your joy may be full" (KJV). The experience of the new birth helps us sort out tragedy from triviality; and it helps us have a joy that circumstances can't take away.

The Question Answered

A friend I worked with was not a Christian. He wanted to know more about the Christian life, for he had had pain in his past and a shadow over his future. After we had talked from time to time, he shook his head and said, "I've lived too bad a life to become a Christian." He couldn't believe God's grace was strong enough to save society's worst as well as its best, and I couldn't convince him otherwise. When I left that job, my friend still was not a Christian. And my inability to clearly explain and convince him of what he needed to believe and do to become a Christian left me with a sinking feeling.

About a year later, I was working in a bookstore, and I got a phone call in the middle of the day. It was my friend Charles. He said, "I became a Christian, and I wanted you to know that I'm enrolled in school and studying for the ministry." God's Spirit had done his work; Charles had responded. And he was able to answer the question: "Yes, I have been born again. God has forgiven me, and I'm happier

than I've ever been in my life." That's what can happen
to everyone who will accept Christ and receive the gift
of life (Rev. 22:17). What is your answer to the question?

Notes

Chapter 1

1. Paul Tournier, *The Seasons of Life* (Richmond, Virginia: John Knox Press, 1967), pp. 9-10.

Chapter 2

1. Ibid., p. 58.
2. Elton Trueblood, *A Place to Stand* (New York: Harper and Row, 1969), p. 97.

Chapter 3

1. Henry Bettenson, ed., *Documents of the Christian Church* (London: Oxford University Press, 1943), p. 14.
2. Robert Baker, *A Summary of Christian History* (Nashville: Broadman Press, 1959), pp. 42, 46.
3. Roland Bainton, *Here I Stand* (Nashville: Abingdon Press, 1950), p. 185.
4. Karl Barth, *Church Dogmatics* (Edinburgh: T. & T. Clark, 1957), Volume 2, Number 2, p. 647.

Chapter 4

1. Charles Colson, *Born Again* (Old Tappan, New Jersey: Chosen Books, 1976), p. viii. (Distributed by Fleming H. Revell Company.)
2. Harry Rimmer, *Flying Worms* (Berne, Indiana: Berne Witness Press, 1948), pp. 33-34.
3. Thomas Harris, *I'm OK, You're OK* (New York: Harper and Row, 1969), pp. xiii-xiv.
4. Tournier, pp. 19, 38, 43.
5. Keith Miller, *The Becomers* (Waco: Word Books, 1973), pp. 132-133.

Chapter 5

1.   F. Scott Fitzgerald, *This Side of Paradise* (New York: Charles Scribner's Sons, 1920), pp. 17-18.

Chapter 6

1.   Jimmy Carter, *Why Not the Best?* (Nashville: Broadman Press, 1975), p. 129.
2.   Leonard Kaufman, *Magazine Journalism and the American Lifestyle*, Chapter 9, 1976, p. 123.
3.   Carter, p. 132.
4.   Jane Ann Webb, "Simplicity" (*event*, Oct. 1973), p. 5.

Chapter 7

1.   Tournier, pp. 45, 53.
2.   Karl Barth, *Dogmatics in Outline* (New York: Harper and Row, 1959), p. 123.
3.   Colson, p. 130.